EDUCATIONAL
LEADERSHIP

EDUCATIONAL LEADERSHIP

Case Studies for Reflective Practice

Carl R. Ashbaugh
Katherine L. Kasten

University of North Florida

Longman

New York & London

Educational Leadership: Case Studies for Reflective Practice

Longman, 95 Church Street, White Plains, N.Y. 10601

Associated companies:
Longman Group Ltd., London
Longman Cheshire Pty., Melbourne
Longman Paul Pty., Auckland
Copp Clark Pitman, Toronto

Executive editor: Raymond T. O'Connell
Production editor: Marie-Josée A. Schorp
Cover design and illustration: Anne M. Pompeo
Production supervisor: Kathleen M. Ryan

Library of Congress Cataloging-in-Publication Data

Ashbaugh, Carl R.
    Educational leadership: case studies for reflective practice/by Carl R.
    Ashbaugh and Katherine L. Kasten.
        p.   cm.
    1. School management and organization—United States—Case
    studies.   2. School administrators—United States—Case studies.
    3. Leadership—Case studies.   4. Values—United States.   I. Kasten,
    Katherine L.   II. Title.
    LB2801.A2A84   1990
    371.2—dc20   89-48555
    ISBN 0-8013-0194-7   CIP

ABCDEFGHIJ-CT-99 98 97 96 95 94 93 92 91 90

We dedicate this book to school people in leadership positions, who daily struggle with the complexities and ambiguities of decision making in organizations.

Genuine freedom ... is intellectual; it rests in the trained power of thought, *in ability to "turn things over," to look at matters deliberately, to judge whether the amount of and kind of evidence requisite for decision is at hand, and if not, to tell where and how to seek such evidence. If ... actions are not guided by thoughtful conclusions, then they are guided by inconsiderate impulse, unbalanced appetite, caprice, or the circumstances of the moment. To cultivate unhindered unreflective external activity is to foster enslavement. . . .*

John Dewey

Contents

Preface

We really started this book in 1984 as we began research on the place of values in administrative decision making. Our primary intents were to describe the kinds of values administrators bring to decision making and to assess the consciousness with which administrators apply those values. As we interviewed school principals and superintendents about difficult decisions they had made, we were struck by the fact that most of those we talked to had not developed habits of reflection. Several described themselves as disinclined to reexamine decisions they had made. Several noted that little in their preparation programs or the routines of their administrative lives encouraged them to reflect upon the ethical or moral dimensions of administration.

As we examined the standard textbooks in educational administration, we found few that dealt explicitly with values and ethics. Kimbrough's monograph (1985) for the American Association of School Administrators, Robinson and Moulton's book on higher education (1985), and Haller and Strike's (1986) introductory text were notable exceptions. We also discovered that few of the published case studies we could locate had the liveliness, immediacy, and complexity of the stories told by the administrators we had interviewed.

We have intended in this book to tell good stories and to capture in them the conflicts and ambiguities of administrative life. We deliberately selected incidents that exemplify conflicts and controversies that appear in school life. Each of the stories is based on an incident that actually occurred, though we have sometimes combined several incidents into a composite story. It would be a mistake, however, to read these cases as if they were factual accounts of actual events. We have fictionalized names, places, and, at times, the sequence of events. We have simplified real life, inferred motivations, and invented conversations. Practicing administrators who have read these cases find that the stories ring true. Aspiring administrators find in them a view of administrative life that is difficult to obtain in textbook accounts of school administration.

However, readers who are satisfied with reading good stories will miss most of the intent of this book. Each of these cases was written around one or more value conflicts. Several should raise issues about ethical and moral practice. It is not essential for readers to have an ethical or philosophical background to study these cases. Nevertheless, they will be difficult to analyze without attention to the values and value conflicts implicit in the statements and actions of the characters.

The field of educational administration is rediscovering the importance of providing frequent and deliberate opportunities for those who aspire to be leaders (as well as those who hope to improve their leadership capabilities) to engage in problem solving in simulations, case analyses, and assessment centers. Such settings combine some of the immediacy of practice with the safety of the classroom, the discussion session, and the laboratory. The development and testing of one's own convictions about the values that should shape life in schools are too important to be left to chance and too critical to be first undertaken in real decisions that impact the lives of others.

This book was written to be used as a stimulus for case analysis of administrative practice. Both those who are naive about administrative life and those who are sophisticated should find these cases interesting and helpful. Readers should test their ideas and values against those of the characters in the cases. But reflection should not always be a solitary process. Understandings, assertions, and convictions need to be tested in interactions with others. Leadership in schools is a social process; the analysis of leadership should be tested in a social arena also. These cases should be debated, discussed, analyzed, and reexamined.

In the chapters that follow we provide a context for case analysis and 62 cases. The first chapter develops the rationale for the use of cases in the study of professional practice. It describes advantages and limitations of the case method and argues for its efficacy in the study of school administration. The second chapter describes a general procedure for the analysis of cases and illustrates it with a case about the termination of a beginning teacher. Chapters 3 through 7 contain the cases, organized in five topical areas. In the Instructor's Guide that accompanies this case book, we suggest questions for use in discussion of the cases, provide alternative organizing categories, and direct instructors to background materials.

We came to this book from different perspectives. Carl Ashbaugh has over thirty years of experience in educational organizations. He has been a teacher, principal, professor of educational administration, dean, and member of the lay governing board for a liberal arts college. Katherine Kasten has been a teacher, teacher leader, professor of educational administration, department chair, and student of administration from the perspective of those governed.

We could not have written this book without the help of teachers, administrators, school board members, professors of educational administration, and others who provided material upon which these stories were based and who gave their reactions to the written stories. We owe them our thanks, though we cannot identify them by name. Four people warrant special recognition. Raymond T. O'Connell, executive editor, Education, for Longman, encouraged us to write the book and made it possible. Lisa Butler and Frank Linn, graduate assistants in the Division of Educational Services and Research at the University of North Florida, were copy editors, critics, and valuable assistants. Joyce Ashbaugh was patient, understanding, and, as always, a wonderful cook.

EDUCATIONAL
LEADERSHIP

CHAPTER 1

The Case Study Method and Educational Administration

Much that is puzzling, exceptional and difficult about those practical questions which are called moral issues has been cleared away for the utilitarian by a policy of abstraction. If I were to defend ... the case against abstract thinking in many matters of moral judgment ... I would do best to tell true stories, drawn from direct experience, of events which have actually involved difficult decisions.

Stuart Hampshire

Those occupying positions of responsibility and leadership in elementary and secondary education have never been without their critics or challengers. Throughout the twentieth century, educational leaders have been exhorted to be more efficient, to demonstrate more accountability and be more effective, to evidence more political savvy, to develop better communication skills, and to become instructional leaders. Most of these expectations are rooted in the conventional wisdom of scientific management and are well documented in classic and contemporary texts in educational administration.

In recent years the field of educational administration has undergone a good deal of ferment, and the basic premises of the scientific management movement have been questioned. When leadership is analyzed through the perspective of scientific management, rational policy guides rational decision making. Scientific management leaves unquestioned the bedrock of values upon which policy rests, values that have too often been unchallenged and uncritically accepted.

1

To suppose that administrators apply policy in an even-handed, cool, objective fashion is naive. The administrative process in education is a highly personal enterprise. Sometimes knowingly, but more often unconsciously, leaders apply their own biases and predilections to daily problems. By ignoring or addressing certain behaviors, by selectively applying rules and regulations, by creatively interpreting certain policies, or by applying policy in an inappropriate fashion simply to expedite a decision and to appear both knowledgeable and decisive, administrators bring their own values into play. While the rational model of scientific management is useful for understanding some of administrative decision making, it cannot capture the complexity of the process through which leaders make decisions that directly or indirectly impinge on the welfare of others and affect them either positively or negatively.

We ask readers of this book to accept as given the importance of values in the decision-making process and to recognize that administration can never be a value-free science. The importance of values in decision making is not regrettable evidence of human frailty but a matter to be described, analyzed, and incorporated into our understanding of administration. Both practicing and aspiring administrators must recognize the inevitable interjection of their personal values in the decisions they make and must be conscious and critical of the value considerations upon which administrative actions are based.

THE USE OF CASES TO STUDY ADMINISTRATION

We have selected the case study approach as most appropriate for the study of administrative decision making because it permits students to examine process and values, action and consequence, in the safety of personal study and group discussion. It is by its very nature a reflective activity, permitting students to examine and reexamine particular administrative actions from a variety of perspectives.

This book has been developed at a time when there is a great deal of criticism of academic programs for educational administrators. In 1964 Culbertson pointed out the "discontinuity between the study of administration and its practice." With remarkable foresight, he suggested that as knowledge about administration increased, this incongruence could well be exacerbated. This may, in fact, have occurred. Thus, the 1987 report of the National Commission on Excellence in Educational Administration recommended that "administration preparation programs should be like those in professional schools which emphasize theoretical and clinical knowledge, applied research, and supervised practice" (p. 20).

The issue of relevance in professional preparation programs is not, of course, unique to the study of educational administration. Donald Schoen (1987) has described the "rigor-or-relevance dilemma" in all professional schools. Common criticisms of professional training programs in general include the remoteness of academic programs from the problems of the field, the passive nature of most instruction, and the failure to present theoretical constructs in ways that are meaningful to students and practicing administrators. Schoen has asserted that "what aspiring practitioners need most to learn, professional schools seem least able to teach" (p. 8).

The case study method stands against these criticisms. For aspiring administrators, case studies provide opportunities to play out the conflicts in administrative decision making without being faced with a lifetime of consequences. Case studies encourage aspiring leaders to examine their own predispositions; to test their own values against the requirements of the organization, the law, and the expectations of constituent groups; and to sort through the competing claims made in any conflict. For practicing administrators, case studies provide tests of their experiences and understandings vis-à-vis new situations and with the luxury of time for reflection and analysis.

History of the Use of Case Studies

Case studies have, for over 100 years, been incorporated into professional preparation programs as one way of bridging the gap between academic knowledge and practice and of teaching that which is most difficult to teach. Originated by Landell in about 1870 in the Harvard Law School, the method was vigorously criticized by those espousing the more traditional techniques of pedagogy. By 1915, however, the case method was the pervasive methodology in the law schools of the country (Culbertson, Jacobson, & Reller, 1960). Circa 1919 the Harvard Business School began to apply the case method, and it is generally recognized to have been the key to that school's preeminent position among the nation's schools of business. Case studies were also used in the Harvard Medical School, and in the 1930s case studies in public administration were developed.

It was not until the 1940s that case materials were developed for preparation programs to prepare school administrators. As described by Culbertson (1964), the early use of case studies was to provide "vicarious administrative experience and to afford opportunities for 'intuitive' decision-making" (p. 325). In the 1960s and 1970s, however, cases were increasingly used to relate concepts and theories to the practice of administration. The University Council for Educational Administration (UCEA) has at various times provided stimulus for the development of cases. If one were to examine current textbooks in the field, however, noting the number and extent of books using case studies, one would hardly conclude that the case method has been widely adopted in the study of administration.

Rationale for the Use of Cases

What can the student of educational leadership expect when studying the complex process of administration through the analysis of cases? Case studies frequently provide more information about the process of administration than the content or knowledge base of the field.

Studying the art and science of educational administration through analysis of cases avoids some of the pitfalls of the rational, scientific approach but has difficulties and pitfalls of its own. In 1987 the authors carried out a study designed to examine the use of case studies as an instructional methodology in programs for preparing school leaders. While the study examined the use of cases from the perspective of professors, the insights obtained may be helpful to students who are new to the use of case methodology.

PROCEDURES IN THE USE OF CASE STUDIES

Cases can be used to accomplish several main purposes. One primary purpose is to help students acquire analytical skills. Determining the central features and essential relations in a case is crucial to problem solving. The analysis of cases helps students think clearly in ambiguous situations. A second purpose is the development of skill in synthesizing information. A student doing a case analysis must combine a variety of elements—time factors, subordination of ideas, propositions and supporting data, ordering of pertinent forces, and separating ideas by level of complexity, to list a few examples. Another purpose for using cases is to promote concept development. Abstractions such as leadership, conflict management, resource allocation, and communication become more concrete and meaningful through the process of case analysis. Theory becomes more relevant as it provides a structure for synthesizing information. Case analysis provides a basis for playing concepts, theories, and other abstractions against concrete situations. A fourth reason for using case instruction is that it provides the opportunity for developing mature judgment and wisdom in a relatively risk-free environment.

Case instruction may also be used to illustrate and apply widely accepted techniques of administration. For example, cases may indicate ways to involve subordinates in decision making. Cases may suggest methods by which administrators can solicit advice from internal and external constituent groups. Case analysis helps to build a repertoire of skills in dealing with nonroutine problems. Finally, cases may be used as one means of socializing neophyte administrators; that is, aspiring administrators begin thinking like the practitioners they wish to become.

Preparing for Case Discussion

The results of a case discussion are more beneficial when both the leader and the participant are prepared. The leader first must select cases having relevance to the central content area(s) of the course. Second, prior to the actual discussion of a particular case, leaders must know what specific topics they wish to cover. Third, leaders must try to anticipate the range of possible related issues that may surface during the discussion and attempt to have on hand illustrative documents, background information, policy statements, and legal rulings that will help bring currency and relevance to the discussion.

Students, of course, have similar responsibilities. Simply reading the assigned case is not enough. A process for systematically thinking through the case content must be employed. One such process will be explained and illustrated in Chapter 2.

Discussing the Case

Students and leaders may become frustrated with the case method because it appears to take so much class time. Involving as many students as possible in the discussion is essential to good pedagogy. Unless this participation is focused and succinct, the discussion can degenerate into the telling of war stories and endless descriptions of "how we do it in my school." Case discussions can rely too much on personal experiences. Even the most targeted case discussion, however, will take longer than developing the same concepts in a traditional lecture format. The final payoff is that case discussions draw students into the class, heighten interest, ensure greater learning through application of key concepts, and bring a sense of reality to the classroom.

Students who are looking for correct answers to the problems illustrated by cases frequently will be frustrated. Students sometimes expect to be told a fail-safe method of handling the case at hand. The reality is that good cases are somewhat ambiguous, with many different avenues of response emerging as genuine possibilities. Even so, a well-discussed case produces some sense of closure or a set of common understandings. Good case analysis "pokes holes in the aura of the science of administration," as one respondent phrased it in our study of case methodology use in educational administration. Further, administrative life is very complex. Through cases, students attain a sense of realism that is often missing in traditional textbooks and lectures. While cases bring a measure of genuineness to the study of administration, however, the perspective of another respondent in our study is worth repeating: "It is not real. There is no substitute for the hot breath of an angry constituent."

Results of Case Discussions

If cases are used well, several benefits result. Students develop analytical skills by learning to think clearly in ambiguous situations. Theory becomes more relevant and students find it useful for providing a more complete understanding of practice. Students vicariously experience a realistic view of administrative life. In addition, discussion of cases and the written analyses that may accompany such study sharpen communication skills, including the ability to listen to others, the ability to see divergent points of view, the ability to speak and write clearly, the ability to imagine and intuit, and the ability to understand one's self.

CONCLUSION

It should be clear that we believe in the efficacy of using case studies. They can do a great deal to add relevance to instruction in educational administration. We hope our readers will enjoy the stories that follow. Their primary purpose, however, is didactic. We have tried to capture the complexity and ambiguity of administrative life in these fictional, but not fictitious, stories and vignettes. Properly used, they should go far toward equipping aspirant administrators to assume leadership roles and helping practicing administrators to reexamine the assumptions and premises behind their own administrative actions.

CHAPTER 2
Analyzing Case Studies

Practically no problem in life ... ever presents itself as a case on which a decision can be taken. What appears at first sight to be elements of the problem rarely are the important relevant things. They are at best symptoms. And often the most visible symptoms are the least revealing ones.

Peter Drucker

This chapter will outline a procedure for analyzing cases. The procedure will be general enough to be applied to most of the cases in this book, though specific techniques will be suggested that may be less generally applicable. Then a case and a sample analysis will demonstrate how the model can be applied.

As was noted in the previous chapter, good cases are accounts of small segments of reality that provide readers with an opportunity to analyze a situation, develop a plan of action, and share their thinking with others in discussions. Some of the cases are open-ended and leave the reader with a difficult problem. Others are more complete stories. A few of them provide readers with more than one possible ending. None is amenable to simple or easy solutions because all of them deal with the complexities of human action within organizations.

Cases are intended to give readers some modest practice in converting theories and general precepts into action. The relationships between theory and the case, however, will rarely be self-evident. Translating theory into the concrete reality of organizational life is difficult ... for everyone.

Students who learn the most from case analysis are those who are willing to take a position even when the situation is ambiguous, when important data are missing, or when relevant background information is not available. Those are the real conditions under which most management decisions are made. Students, like managers, must be willing to commit themselves to a recommendation even when they are unsure of the reactions that others will have to their position. Students who have prepared a well-thought-out justification for their recommendations should be willing to test those recommendations against the reactions of colleagues.

Using cases to study administrative practice entails developing skill in analytical processes. Students who are given a case as part of a class assignment typically proceed through several steps. They read the case, analyze it, and arrive at an action recommendation or an evaluation of actions already taken. Then they usually participate in a group discussion of the case, comparing their analysis with those of other group members. Written analysis of cases may be assigned, and students may be asked to present their analysis to the group.

Each of these steps will shortly be discussed at some length, but they do not begin to capture the complexity and difficulty of case analysis. There are no right or wrong answers to any good case—within reason, of course. While there is unlikely to be one correct solution to any case, there are less satisfactory solutions and alternatives that may be judged illegal or unethical.

PROCEDURES IN CASE ANALYSIS

Reading the Case

First, read the case quickly, much as you would any story, to get a general sense of the content and to become familiar with the principal actors. Then read it again, this time underlining key parts and making marginal notes when ideas occur to you. After reading the case twice, you may find it helpful to decide whether this is a case that calls for a recommendation to overcome a problem or one that asks for the evaluation of a decision already made.

Identifying the Central Problem

Next, identify the central problem. Frame it in a sentence or two. You may want to write it down. In most cases there will be one central, major, or primary problem. Identifying the problem may seem easy, but life situations don't present themselves with clearly labeled designations such as "problem." In the cases you read, look for instances of behavior that seem atypical, that signal conflicts among characters, that precipitate change or perpetuate stagnation, or that indicate other stresses that tax the resources of the organization. You can identify problems by contrasting things as they exist with things as you believe they should be. As you learn more about organizational structures, about individual needs and motivations, and about group processes, you should become more astute and skilled in your analysis of problems.

To test whether what you have identified is, in fact, a key problem, ask yourself whether the losses incurred from failure to deal with this problem successfully would be substantial. Would such failure have a negative impact on the organization and its members? Are the losses likely to be long-term rather than short-lived?

Identifying Secondary Problems

Although a secondary problem may precipitate a crisis in an organization, avoid mistaking secondary or subordinate problems for the primary problem. For example, organizations are prone to problems related to inadequate communication, but inadequate communication is usually not the central problem. George may fail to pass on information to Mary; that's inadequate communication. However, George's failure may be the result of a desire to defend his own turf or a fear that Mary knows more than he does. Unless the central problem is identified and dealt with, it will occur again and again, although the particular manifestations may change.

Secondary problems cannot be ignored, of course. Part of the case analysis process is to document these secondary problems and to indicate how they are related to the central problem of the case.

Finding Supporting Information

Through some coding process, identify the information in the case that is relevant to the central problem and to each of the secondary problems. Though none of the cases in the chapters that follow are very lengthy, a few deliberately contain some less relevant information. Check the evidence you select for plausibility by making a series of comparisons. Compare each piece of evidence against other evidence that supports the problem. Evidence should be internally consistent. It should be plausible in comparison with your personal experiences, and it should be plausible given what is known about the history of the organization. In selecting evidence, use assumptions judiciously. If your selection rests upon an assumption, question whether the assumption is reasonable and speculate about the effects on your analysis should your assumption prove to be inaccurate.

Developing Alternative Solutions

The next step is to develop alternative courses of action that would address the central problem. Most case analysis fails to generate enough alternatives to ensure that the most effective or appropriate alternative is being considered.

One way to generate alternatives is to engage in private brainstorming—listing as many alternatives as you can. You might recall how you and others you know have solved similar problems, you might do research to discover how others have addressed similar problems, or you might simply let your mind focus on the issue at hand and allow it to function as creatively as possible.

If the central problem concerns desire for change or resistance to change, *force field analysis* may be employed as a systematic way to determine a solution. Through this technique, positive and negative influences that have created an equilibrium mitigating against a solution to the problem or a resolution of the conflict can be identified. After identifying the problem, try to identify the forces that are operating to bring about a solution (driving forces) and those that are striving to maintain the status quo (restraining forces). (See Figure 2.1.) These two sets of forces provide the raw material from which viable alternatives may be framed. A solution is most likely to result when an imbalance occurs between the sum of these two sets of forces and a new equilibrium results. One may increase the driving forces or seek to diminish the restraining forces. The strategy most likely to produce positive results is to figure out ways to alleviate the restraining forces. It makes sense, then, to begin with the restraining forces most amenable to change, specifically the ones that are most modifiable.

It is sometimes valuable to list two sets of alternatives: those that were available to the key actor(s) in the case before the problem developed, and those that are currently available. This technique has heuristic value for those studying leadership because it forces consideration of what might have been done to prevent the problem in the first place. Also, it is instructive to compare the set of constraints and opportunities present in

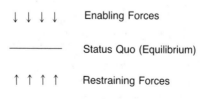

↓ ↓ ↓ ↓   Enabling Forces

——————   Status Quo (Equilibrium)

↑ ↑ ↑ ↑   Restraining Forces

Figure 2.1.

the organization before the problem developed with the set of circumstances after the problem surfaced.

Evaluating Alternative Solutions

Once the alternatives have been identified, subject each to some sort of scrutiny. The following questions may be helpful for assessing the available alternatives.

1. Is the alternative consistent with the organization's policies, objectives, and procedures?
2. How much will it cost in time, money, or other organizational resources?
3. Can the alternative be effective in the time available to solve the problem?
4. What is the probability of success?
5. What will be the likely level of support from organization members and external constituents?
6. What values will be signaled if this alternative is chosen for implementation?

Securing the answers to these questions may be accomplished through a procedure drawn from accounting called the T-account, listing of advantages in one column and disadvantages in another (see Edge & Coleman, 1978). If a T-account is developed for each alternative, the process becomes iterative and the disadvantages of one alternative may appear as the advantages of another. We recommend selective use of this procedure (see Figure 2.2).

Selecting the Preferred Alternative

The final step in evaluation is to choose the alternative most likely to solve the problem or bring about the desired change. If a decision has already been made, the analyst will, instead, evaluate the alternative chosen

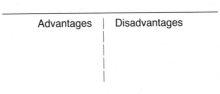

Figure 2.2.

against those that were available at the time the decision was made, and perhaps suggest a better option. Although the choice of alternative will inevitably be a subjective judgment, it will be a judgment based on careful analysis. The decision maker can have confidence in the final decision.

Planning for Implementation

The rational choice of an alternative is not the end of the case analysis. No alternative is without a downside, and each carries with it certain risks. For example, the alternative selected may require others to change the way they go about their work or the way they feel about themselves and the organization. Change in behavior may have to precede, not follow, change in attitude. The capabilities of organization members may limit the successful implementation of the alternative selected. The plan may not be sufficiently flexible to accommodate the inevitable needs for revision as implementation proceeds. At the same time, searching for the perfect solution would mean that no action would ever be taken.

Although it is impossible to find a plan without faults or to anticipate all contingencies, a plan for implementation should be developed that compensates for the predictable limitations of the alternative selected and that provides for some flexibility. In analysis of some of the cases that follow, it will be useful to develop fully an implementation plan, including a list of activities, identification of responsible parties, a suggested time-line, and measures of intended outcomes.

The case analysis procedure described above is summarized below.

Summary of Case Analysis Procedure

1. Read the case quickly and then again carefully to decide whether the case analysis will require developing a recommendation or evaluating a decision that has already been made.
2. Identify the central problem.
3. Identify secondary problems.
4. Locate evidence to support identification of the central problem and the secondary problems.
5. Develop alternative solutions through brainstorming or force field analysis.
6. Evaluate the alternatives proposed.
7. Select the alternative most likely to solve the problem or bring about the desired change, or suggest a better option.
8. Plan for implementation.

Writing the Case Analysis

A written case analysis does not reveal the messy, complex thought process that has preceded the report. During the preparation of the case, it may become evident that one has misidentified the problem only when it becomes necessary to generate alternative solutions. False starts, dead ends, and recycling efforts are generally ignored in the written report and the analysis is presented not as one did it, but as one would want to read it. The written analysis should be rational, sequential, and orderly, even though the process of analysis was not.

In the next section a case will be presented for analysis to illustrate how the process described above can be used. Not all of the cases in this book will lend themselves to the complete analysis as described. The analyst will need to be selective and apply those parts of the procedure that make sense in the content of a specific case.

CASE 2.1: TERMINATING
A YOUNG, ANGRY TEACHER

"Nick, I'm sorry," Principal Jack Hawthorne continued, "but I've decided that your teaching contract must be terminated at the end of this semester. It's the only thing I can do, given your reactions to our attempts to help you. I wish it had worked out differently."

Nicholas Mazzoni barely responded. He was young, muscular, dressed more casually than the other teachers at Edison Senior High School. "Work clothes," Jack thought. "Nick always looks like he's just fixed a car or loaded a truck."

In the five months that Jack had known Nick, the chip on Nick's shoulder had not moved. Hiring Nick, a beginning teacher straight from the south side of Milwaukee, to teach social studies at very suburban Whitman High had been a risk. Jack had known that when he did it. But the risk didn't seem as serious when Jack found out that Nick was engaged to Lily Thompson, the daughter of Phil Thompson, an elementary school principal in the district and one of Jack's best friends.

Nick was smart and seemed enthusiastic, but he was clearly out of place here. As Jack learned more about Nick, he found out that Nick had lived all of his life in the city, had attended the urban junior college and then the university, and had been the first in his family to get a college degree. His roots were in the working-class immigrant neighborhoods of Milwaukee's south side, and Nick let everyone know it. Nick hated the suburb and would never have moved out of the city if it hadn't been for Lily.

Complaints about Nick had begun within the first month of school in September. When the social studies department chair, Mildred Robbins, had tried to work with him, he had rejected her help out of hand. Nick had refused to follow the course outline for the junior year American history course, saying that it did not recognize the contributions of ethnic minorities and women to the history of the country. Nick had told Mildred that it was his job to "tell the truth about American history," especially, he said, as it related to the working class and people of color. Before September was over, Mildred had reported to Jack that "we may have a serious problem on our hands." Jack had asked to be kept informed and had suggested that Mildred keep a record of her conversations with Nick, in addition to her usual classroom visits.

In October complaints from parents began, slowly at first. Jack had tried talking to Nick himself, then had sought advice from Phil Thompson about how to approach Nick. Phil was not much help. He described Nick as "good-hearted," "stubborn," and "very smart." Phil didn't seem to think the problems Jack described were serious. Nick, he thought, would get a better sense of his students as he became more experienced.

For a while it looked as if Phil might be right. Three weeks went by without incident. Jack observed one of Nick's classes and found it stimulating. Students were arguing with Nick about his interpretation of history, and he was forcing them to back up their statements with facts and to explain inferences. Then, at the end of October, Jack got a call from a local businessman who said his daughter had come home from school emotionally distraught. When she had answered a question in American history, Nick had told her that her answer was "stupid" and "a perfect example" of the kind of "intellectual myopia" that could be expected of "Whitman school cheerleaders." Jack spoke to Mildred later that same day, and she told him that things had not changed much. In fact, her earlier concerns had intensified. She said she had received complaints from other students, who had reported verbal abuse of the sort Jack had just heard about. Mildred herself had never seen anything like that when she observed Nick teach, but she was aware that he frequently raised his voice, almost shouting at the students in his classes.

After his conversation with Mildred, Jack decided it was time to do something. He called the Personnel Office that week. The reaction he got was not encouraging. Pete Rawlings, the personnel director, asked whether there was any way to work with Nick until the end of the school year. "You know how hard it is to find permanent replacements," Pete explained. When Jack told Pete he didn't think it was possible, Pete's response was, "We really wish you'd try." That had ended the conversation.

Jack tried once more to meet with Nick in early November. He was blunt and laid out the problems. Nick didn't follow the established curriculum. He had rejected advice about his teaching from the department chair and from the social studies supervisor. Students had complained; parents had complained.

Nick repeated what he had said before. In his best professional judgment, he said, he was doing the right thing. "These kids," he said, "have been too sheltered. They have sterile histories, and they don't know what life is about. Sure they feel threatened because I challenge their deep-seated, but wrong, beliefs. They're almost adults. They can handle it, and they'll know more about history as a result."

Finally, in frustration, Jack told Nick that he wanted the complaints to stop, that Nick would have to adjust to his students enough to gain their support.

The complaints did not stop. During the Thanksgiving break, Jack spent some time thinking through the problem. He laid it out rationally. Here was a first-year teacher, engaged to a friend's daughter, who seemed to be offering to students a missing and badly needed perspective on American history. Jack knew some people would think that Nick was being fired for his ideology. What's more, firing a first-year teacher in mid year would be seen by central office as Jack's failure, evidence of poor hiring and ineffective leadership, if only because it would create a problem for the district administrators.

On the other hand, Nick had been difficult to work with. He had refused to use the approved curriculum. He used unorthodox teaching methods that sometimes left students confused, embarrassed, and angry. Several parents had complained about Nick to the assistant principals, the counselors, and Jack. Nick simply refused to bend.

Jack finally decided that he had no choice but to let Nick go. Jack knew he would be seen by some as weak and faint hearted for choosing to get rid of Nick, but he was convinced that Nick should not be permitted to use the classroom as a forum for his personal anger.

And that was what had brought him to this moment. Nick's reaction was as cold and dark as the winter sky outside Jack's office. Finally Nick looked at Jack, cleared his throat, and said he wasn't surprised. "I knew," Nick said, "that the deck was stacked against me when I walked into this school. I've tried to be true to myself and to my discipline. These are young adults, not kids. You are ruining my career as a teacher because you want to protect them as they've been protected all their lives."

"I'm sorry you see it that way, Nick," Jack had responded. "I do think you could be a good teacher, maybe someplace where you felt more at home. I'll be happy to write a reference for you."

"Don't do me any favors," Nick replied, as he pushed himself out of the chair and turned to leave Jack's office.

ANALYSIS OF "TERMINATING A YOUNG, ANGRY TEACHER"

The case is a classic illustration of conflicts between the rights and responsibilities of the individual and those of the group. Reread the summary checklist on page 12 before proceeding with your analysis. The boldfaced words below refer to key words in that checklist.

Because the case concludes after Jack Hawthorne has terminated Nick Mazzoni, we will need to **evaluate** the appropriateness of that action.

The **central problem** in the case is an inflexible teacher with an unacceptable teaching style. The problem is significant because of the assumed effects that Nick's continuing to teach at the school will have on the cohesiveness of the school and support from parents in the community.

A good deal of evidence about Nick's inflexibility is included in the case. Nick refused to follow the course outline. He rejected the help of the social studies department chairman. He was vocal in his conviction that only he tells the truth about American history. At the same time, we have evidence in the case that Nick's teaching style is unacceptable in this community. Some parents have complained; at least one student was emotionally upset as a result of Nick's class. The only evidence presented to counterbalance this description of the problem is Hawthorne's rather positive evaluation after he observed Nick's teaching.

Secondary problems relevant to the case include Nick's appearance, his status as a first-year teacher, his feeling of displacement in the community, the friendship between Jack Hawthorne and Phil Thompson, and the reluctance of central administration to support Hawthorne in his efforts to terminate Mazzoni.

We have assumed in this analysis that Nick's teaching approach is rooted in his background and in his deep-seated anger against those suburbanites who are insulated from problems faced by the urban underclass, rather than defensible convictions about the best pedagogical approach to instruction. This assumption seems justifiable given that Nick is a first-year teacher and the considerable **evidence** of his anger. At the same time, the accuracy of this assumption may not be crucial because Nick's behavior is unacceptable regardless of the explanation for it.

Several **alternatives** were available to Hawthorne at the time he decided to terminate Nick.

1. He could have waited until the end of the semester to terminate Nick, although he might have given Nick immediate notice of his intention.
2. He could have continued to try to work with Nick, encouraging him to develop alternative teaching methods.

3. He could have enlisted Phil's help in socializing Nick to observe the mores of the community.
4. He could have delayed a decision while he quietly and unobtrusively assessed the extent and degree of dissension with Nick's teaching.
5. He could have developed a specific plan for remediation and sought Nick's agreement with it.

Each of these alternatives was **evaluated** by balancing the advantages and disadvantages. A discussion of one will serve to illustrate the process.

A decision to continue to work with Nick in developing several teaching strategies has several advantages. Working with him will provide continuity for the students in his classes and may allow him to become a teacher who can contribute to the profession. Advantages to Hawthorne include minimizing the involvement of central office in building-level personnel problems, avoiding a possible personnel hearing, not needing to hire a new teacher, and maintaining cordial relations with the Thompsons.

Continuing to work with Nick also has disadvantages. The situation may deteriorate further and student and parent complaints may increase. The department chair's support for Jack may diminish. Even if Nick agrees to cooperate with these efforts, there is no guarantee of success.

Given what we know from the case and what we assume Jack Hawthorne knew, the decision to terminate Nick was premature. Although that decision is likely to produce a less stressful classroom environment for the students and will eliminate the need for Mildred and Jack to monitor Nick's performance, the decision has catastrophic personal and professional consequences for Nick. His career as a teacher could well be finished. Because of the serious consequences attendant to this decision, Jack erred in deciding to terminate Nick at this time. In addition to the consequences for Nick, the decision may have unfortunate consequences for Hawthorne. The community may have been sent the message that all it takes to terminate a teacher is one complaint by an influential citizen.

A **better option** would have been for Jack quietly and unobtrusively to collect more evidence. If he had done this, he would have had a better sense of the level of support for Nick's instructional methodology among students, teachers, and the community. Though Hawthorne concluded from his own observation of Nick's teaching that Nick had something valuable to offer students, he chose to ignore that evidence in his decision. A search for more data could be viewed as one way to protect the rights of an individual against unreasonable, and possibly limited, dissension. One disadvantage of this choice is that it leaves the problem unresolved, delaying what may be an inevitable decision. Further, if Jack chooses this alternative, he may appear indecisive and he and the department chair will undoubtedly need to continue their intensive supervision of Nick. In spite of these disadvantages, we believe that this is the best alternative. On balance, the potential harm to students, which would justify moving expeditiously to terminate Nick, is outweighed by the certain harm to Nick if he is terminated immediately. Taking additional time to gather solid, pertinent data will permit Hawthorne to make a more defensible decision.

CONCLUSION

You may disagree with our analysis of "Terminating a Young, Angry Teacher" and be able to develop a more compelling argument for another alternative, but we hope that you understand the process of case analysis described.

In our own analysis of the case, we followed the process outlined above. The process, however, was iterative. For example, as we identified evidence to support the central problem, we revised our statement of significance to focus on the probable effects of Nick's continued employment rather than the indications of conflict we had initially listed. As we built T-accounts for alternatives that we had listed, we discovered the alternative we eventually selected as preferable. In your analysis, you may find yourself moving similarly between various parts of the process. Our written case analysis, however, contains no indication that these revisions in our thinking occurred.

In the chapters that follow, you will find over 60 stories of administrative decision making. We hope you will enjoy reading them. More important, we hope that your analyses of them will be interesting, provocative, and helpful to you as you study the complexities of educational leadership.

CHAPTER 3

Cases in Managing People

Each administrative decision carries with it a restructuring of a human life; this is why administration at its heart is the resolution of moral dilemmas.

William Foster

CASE 3.1: INSERVICE FOR TEACHERS
IN GREAT PLAINS SCHOOL DISTRICT

Margaret was not sure why inservice days always seemed to be scheduled when the weather was nicest outside. Though she had been teaching school for over two years now, she always felt a little like a student again on inservice days, forced to sit inside and listen to a lecturer when she would much rather be jogging or sitting in the sun or taking her own children to the beach. At least the speaker, a woman from a university in a neighboring state, was talking about something she herself was interested in. She had heard a lot about mastery learning, and she supposed it was time she really knew something about it. And having some inservice time meant that she could get some grades recorded for the papers that she had accumulated during the previous week.

Margaret looked for a seat in the student cafeteria that was close to the window and far enough back from the speaker so that she could discreetly spread out her grade book and her papers. Margaret filled out the form that verified her presence at the session, a procedure she resented so much that for one session a year before she had submitted a fictitious name. No one had ever followed up on it, but she always wondered if anyone in central office had noticed. The room filled up quickly; people helped themselves to cookies and coffee and took seats at various tables around the room.

About ten minutes after the session was scheduled to begin, the director of elementary education rose to introduce the speaker. "Okay, ladies and gentlemen," the director began, "let's all put on our listening hats."

"Come off it," Margaret thought. "That woman will never learn to treat adults like adults." The director told a joke that was mildly amusing, read from the speaker's résumé, and finally let the speaker begin.

Margaret was recording her students' grades while listening to the speaker when the elementary supervisor for her building, Roberta Martinson, tapped her on the shoulder. "Please put your papers away," Roberta whispered.

"Okay," Margaret whispered back. "I'm sorry. I didn't realize I was bothering anyone." Margaret discreetly stacked up her papers, stuffed them in her tote bag, and listened to the rest of the speaker's presentation.

She didn't think any more about the incident until two days later when her principal, Steve Klein, asked her to drop by his office. Steve shut the door and began, "Margaret, I just received a memo from Mrs. Martinson about you." He handed it to her to read:

> Mr. Klein, it is with some regret that I am writing to inform you that one of your staff members, Margaret Lynch, was correcting papers during our inservice presentation on mastery learning earlier this week. The district brought in a highly respected (and expensive) speaker for this presentation. I feel I cannot let Mrs. Lynch's rude behavior go unnoticed. I hope that you will talk with her about this problem.

Margaret was stunned. She surely had not meant to be rude. She had put the papers away when asked, and she had even apologized. What had she done to cause Mrs. Martinson to respond in this vindictive manner?

CASE 3.2: CHILD ABUSE AT LINCOLN ELEMENTARY SCHOOL

As Judith Larson, the school nurse, and Nancy examined Samantha, they had no doubts that the child had been beaten. Nancy had seen children with bruises before in her three years as an elementary school principal, but she would never get used to the sight, particularly when she suspected, as she did here, that the parent was at fault. She had never, however, had to face a case in which one of her own employees was the parent. Regina, Samantha's mother, worked in the cafeteria at Lincoln School. That certainly didn't make it any easier.

Both state law and school district policy required Nancy to report possible cases of child abuse immediately. She walked to her office and dialed the number of the student personnel case worker for her school. Martin Bunson answered and said he would be right over.

Nancy called Joan Anderson, Samantha's teacher, into the hallway outside her classroom. Joan had reported the bruises to Nancy earlier that morning. "I'm pretty sure Samantha has been beaten," Nancy told her, "and Judith agrees."

"I'm so sorry," Joan replied. "If Regina is at fault, she will be heartbroken when she finds out that Samantha will be placed in a foster home. Much as she gets angry at Samantha, I know she loves her. You know, I started paying close attention a couple of days ago when Samantha told me that her mother and her boyfriend had a big fight and that he had moved out of the house."

"Samantha's in Judith's office now. We'll keep her there until Martin Bunson gets here."

"Okay," Joan said. "Let me know if there's anything I can do."

Martin took charge when he walked into the building. He said that he would take Samantha with him and arrange a place for her to stay that evening. Martin told Nancy that the child welfare people would contact Samantha's mother and that Nancy should stay clear of the mother if at all possible. "Stay out of the cafeteria; stay out of her way. Let the welfare people handle it," Martin said. "They deal with these cases all the time." He left the building with Samantha holding his hand.

Nancy couldn't stay out of the cafeteria at lunch time. She was the supervisor, and people expected her to be there. As soon as Joan's class began to enter the cafeteria, Nancy knew she had made a mistake. Regina would obviously notice that Samantha was not with her class, and she would want to know why.

Nancy was not prepared for Regina's anger when she told her, in the privacy of the principal's office, that Samantha was with a student case worker and that arrangements were being made for her to stay with another family until Regina could meet with the child welfare people and work out her problems with her child. Regina swore, kicked the desk and the door, told Nancy she would beat her up the first opportunity she had, and that Nancy had better stay out of her neighborhood. "Mrs. Fawley, don't you know," she asked Nancy, "that when a child don't clean her room, she's got to be punished? I didn't hit her hard. Just enough to let her know that I meant what I said." Regina finally calmed down enough to call

Martin Bunson's office, and Nancy listened as she made arrangements for him to pick her up and take her to the welfare office downtown.

When Regina left her office, Nancy slumped into her chair and stared out the window. The child had needed help, and she had arranged for that help. If that was all there was to it, why did she feel so bad?

CASE 3.3: THE AFFAIR

Principal Donna Reisher hung up the phone quietly, though she had really wanted to throw it against the wall. It wasn't that she had received answers she hadn't expected from Doug Smith, director of personnel for Warren County School District. Donna just hadn't been given the answers she wanted. She had called to check on the policy for termination of a tenured teacher for cause. Though the policy was clear in regard to reasons for termination, the procedures to be followed were vague. And Donna had asked about the district's policy on the use of lie detector tests. Doug had told her that he didn't recommend it, that she would be on shaky ground if the test were done and the case were ever appealed.

"The case . . . ." It seemed strange to refer to Jim Ramsey and the accusations against him as "the case." Ramsey was a social studies teacher at Edison High School, married, three children, a teacher for ten years, very popular with students and respected by faculty, the last person she would have wished this kind of problem on.

Though Donna had serious doubts about the credibility of the student, Ellen Carrigan had refused to back off her story. Mr. and Mrs. Carrigan and Ellen had been in her office early that morning. Mrs. Carrigan was in tears, but she struggled to register their complaint. She said that she had discovered a couple of days earlier that Ellen was taking birth control pills. When she had confronted Ellen, Ellen had at first refused to talk about it, had locked herself in her room, but had finally told Mrs. Carrigan that she was in love with her social studies teacher, Jim Ramsey, and that they had been sleeping together for several months. Donna's first concern had been to protect Jim. She could easily imagine that Ellen was in love with her teacher; that was common enough, even among the relatively sophisticated students at Edison High. And Donna could easily imagine that Ellen was sleeping with someone, though she doubted it was Jim Ramsey. So she had decided to deal with the problem directly, and she had sent a message to Ramsey asking him to come to her office immediately.

The meeting between the Carrigans and Ramsey had been strained and difficult. When Ramsey entered, he saw Ellen and blanched. While Ramsey denied the accusations, Donna noticed that he had trouble looking at her or the Carrigans and that he was visibly shaken. Ellen insisted she was telling the truth, and the Carrigans stood by her. Finally, Donna asked Jim to leave the office, and she asked the Carrigans to give her some time to check out their story. She promised to call them with more information by the end of the day.

She had sought out Grace Allison, a counselor and trusted member of the staff. Donna asked Grace whether she knew anything about Ellen Carrigan that Donna should be aware of. Grace said that Ellen was an average student who passed most of her classes but seemed uninterested in school for the most part. She said there had always been rumors about Ellen, that other students were convinced she was one of the most sexually active girls at Edison. When Donna asked in the most general way she could, Grace said she had not heard anything about Ellen being involved with a teacher.

That's when Donna had called County Personnel Director Doug Smith and described the situation to him: a student with a questionable reputation refuses to back down from her story that she has been having an affair with a respected married teacher. Donna told Smith that she was concerned. While she had at first been convinced that the student was lying, she was no longer so sure. It was possible that the student's story was true.

Donna decided to talk to Jim Ramsey again. She called him back to her office and laid out the problem as she saw it. Though Doug had not encouraged her to do so, she recommended to Jim that he volunteer for a lie detector test. She told him that she was convinced that the test would support his story and they could put this whole incident to rest quickly. She was dismayed when Ramsey refused. He did not elaborate. He only repeated, "I can't do that."

Donna had promised to contact the Carrigans by the end of the day. She had intended to phone them, but they returned to her office before she was ready for them. They hadn't changed their story or their insistence that the teacher must be punished. Mrs. Carrigan was no longer in tears; her face had the hard, firm determination of a person eager for retribution. As Donna escorted them into her office, she had no idea what she could do to resolve this problem.

CASE 3.4: THE SUPERINTENDENT'S CONTRACT

The Board of Education for the Meridian Public Schools was typical of boards in most urban areas. Board members were inclined to represent special interests and areas of the city rather than the school district, and it was difficult to reach consensus on virtually any issue. Tom Kilgore, superintendent of schools in Meridian, was no longer sure why he had wanted so much to be superintendent of a large city school district, and he was not at all sure whether it was worth it now that he had the job. Once again the board was deliberating; this time it was about his contract. It was ironic that the current issue of *Executive Educator* had just arrived with a cover story on the tenure of big city superintendents.

Kilgore knew that board members were aware of the effort he put into the job. He worked long hours. He was usually in the office by 5:30 A.M., and he frequently did not finish his workday until 9:00 or 10:00 P.M. Though he had never asked them to, he noticed that the administrators began getting to work earlier in the morning as well. He probably worked harder than most superintendents. He had been employed by the district for several years, but he also knew from the article he just read that his three years as the top administrator were about the average tenure for school superintendents in large school districts.

Board members frequently talked about vague concepts such as "management style," "relations with the community," and "personal qualities" when they discussed his work with him. The problem was that they never agreed about what they wanted from him in any of those areas, and they were hard pressed to tell him what he was doing wrong or what he could do better.

Though he no longer found much joy in his work, he couldn't imagine what he would do next after having been superintendent of the largest and most complex district in the state. He had been offered other jobs in large districts in other states, but he was reluctant to start over, to build all the connections that made the superintendent's job possible. He thought about retirement, about fishing and spending time with his grandchildren. Retiring at 55 years of age was not a prospect he had thought he would ever seriously consider when he was a younger man, eager to get to the top.

Two weeks later, after two special sessions lasting over three hours each, the Board of Education announced that Kilgore's contract would be renewed for another year. When Board President Joe McMurray was asked by the reporter for the local newspaper what the board's evaluation of Kilgore had been, he had replied, "Since we renewed his contract another year, I feel the evaluation was more than satisfactory." That and a 5 percent salary increase were the thanks Kilgore had received for his work. Frankly, fishing was looking better to him all the time.

CASE 3.5: LIVING IN SIN

Administrators do not always agree on what constitutes best administrative practice. In fact, what is best in one situation or context may not be effective in another. In the case that follows, two superintendents react very differently to the same kind of letter.

Superintendent Franklin's Reaction

She read the letter one more time:

> Dear Superintendent Franklin:
>
> For some time now, we have been wanting to bring a difficult matter to your attention. You are probably not aware of this, but two of the teachers from J. H. Morrison Junior High, Ms. Jones and Mr. Green, are living together in an apartment in Valley View subdivision. Several students from Morrison also live in the apartment building, and they are very much aware of *what is going on*, if you know what we mean! We believe that this sort of behavior is highly inappropriate for our teachers and contrary to moral principles we try to instill in our children.
>
> We want to know what you are going to do about this disgraceful situation.
>
> > Sincerely,
> > Concerned Parents for Moral Action

Michele Franklin read through the several signatures that followed. She recognized most of them, and she wondered if she had a problem on her hands. She made a note to call Beth Schneider, the principal at Morrison, to talk to her about it.

Meanwhile, Michele had a message to call Scott Flannery, one of the signers of the letter. She knew what she would tell Scott . . . what she told everyone in cases like this: "You come into my office on Monday morning at 8:00 o'clock. I'll have the teachers here, and you make the same accusations to them that you're making to me. Then we'll talk about it."

She knew that Flannery would back down. That had been her experience in every case like this in her ten years as superintendent.

Superintendent Bernard's Reaction

He read the letter one more time:

> Dear Superintendent Bernard:
>
> For some time now, we have been wanting to bring a difficult matter to your attention. You are probably not aware of this, but two of the teachers from Don Bosco Junior High, Ms. Donaldson and Mr. Garri-

son, are living together in an apartment in Hidden Valley subdivision. Several students from Don Bosco also live in the apartment building, and they are very much aware of *what is going on*, if you know what we mean! We believe that this sort of behavior is highly inappropriate for our teachers and contrary to moral principles we try to instill in our children.

We want to know what you are going to do about this disgraceful situation.

Sincerely,
Concerned Don Bosco Parents

Mike Bernard read through the signatures that followed. He recognized most of them, and he wondered if he had a problem on his hands. He made a note to call Wanda Dickson, the principal at Don Bosco Junior High, to talk to her about it.

Meanwhile, Mike had a message to call Steve Gamble, one of the signers of the letter. He knew what he'd tell Steve . . . what he told everyone in cases like this: "Thank you for your concern. We're aware of the problem. We are looking into it."

He had a chance to see Wanda later in the week. She confirmed that Rachel Donaldson and Charles Garrison had been spending a lot of time together, even around school, but both were single and young and she hadn't been concerned about it. She even remembered thinking she was happy they had found each other; it was hard to keep good young teachers in a small town like Spring Lake. As far as she knew, their relationship with each other had not affected their teaching. She had heard some seventh graders teasing Rachel about Charles the week before at volleyball practice, but Rachel had handled it well.

Mike knew what the school district's lawyer would tell him: If their actions aren't interfering with their work, you don't have a case. Still, Mike had lived in Spring Lake a long time. He knew that small towns could be tough places for young teachers, and he hated to see these two, obviously promising, young people get themselves in trouble. He decided to talk to them about the letter.

Case 3.5: Part Two

Now that he had Rachel and Charles in his office, Mike wasn't quite sure what to say. He cleared his throat and began, "I've asked you both to stop by because I received a letter last week that concerned both of you. I just wanted you to know about it." He handed each of them a copy of the letter. He had removed the signatures.

"I support your right to private lives apart from your work for Spring Lake Public Schools," he continued, "but I also want you to be aware of these parents' concerns and to think about what you might do to make this situation better."

"You mean we shouldn't be living together," Charles responded.

"I didn't say that. Maybe you would find it easier to teach in this community if you didn't teach at the same school, or if you lived together but not in Spring Lake, or if you got married. I can't tell you how to live your private lives, and I support your rights to privacy. But I do think that you have a right to know that some parents in the community are concerned. Given what I have heard from Wanda Dickson, you are both very effective teachers. We'd like to see you stay in Spring Lake."

"You mean that you talked to Wanda about this?" Rachel asked.

"Yes, of course, I did."

"How could you do that?" she continued.

"The respect and support that parents have for teachers in this school district concerns me, and the respect and support that parents have for teachers at Don Bosco concerns Wanda. Though you may not like to see things this way, teachers' private lives do sometimes become public issues. I wouldn't like to see that happen here."

"What should we do?" Charles asked.

"I don't know," Mike replied. "I think you should think about it, talk to each other, decide what you can do. I just thought it was only fair that you be informed about the letter and the concerns that some parents have expressed."

CASE 3.6: SUPERVISING THE CUSTODIAL CREW

Frank didn't look forward to this meeting with the custodial crews. Though he was officially the custodians' supervisor as principal of the junior high school, he often felt he wasn't really the person they looked to for direction or orders. In fact, when Jim Lockert, the head engineer on the evening shift, had felt that his crew was overworked, he should have reported that to Frank; instead, Jim had taken his complaints to George McIsaac at the central office, and McIsaac had worked out his own way of dealing with the problems. Frank assumed that was what this meeting would be about. He wasn't sure whether McIsaac would be there or not.

When Frank arrived at the conference room, most of the members of the day and night crew were already there. As the last few came in, Frank poured himself a cup of coffee and took a couple of cookies. Pete Stapleton, the day engineer, had called the meeting and would chair it. McIsaac was not in the room. Pete was seated at a table in the front of the room, with papers spread out in front of him. Frank sat down next to Pete.

The members of the day and night crews took seats facing Pete and Frank. Pete began by telling the group that he wanted to read to them the new work assignments that McIsaac had developed. As Pete read through the assignments, members of the crew were obviously getting upset. Several guys were shifting in their chairs, and two women in the center of the room began whispering loudly to each other. When Pete finished, Harold Jefferson raised his hand. "What," Harold asked, "exactly is the reason for these changes?"

Pete tried to explain, "McIsaac and some other people in central office felt that some of the custodians here were overworked, especially on the night shift, and they wanted to divide up the work more fairly."

Harold responded, "Nobody asked me."

"Or me," added Joyce Martin. "Nobody ever asks me."

"Look," Pete said, "we fight much too much with each other. We should be embarrassed that we can't get along and help each other out instead of constantly worrying about who is working harder."

"I agree," added Jim Lockert, "but then you've got to make sure that your people do the work that they're assigned. Otherwise, my crew ends up with more than . . . ."

"Some days," Frank interrupted, "we all have more than we can handle. The day crew can't predict when they'll have emergencies or be asked to do extra, and neither can the night crew. The point is that we're all one team, and we've got to start thinking of ourselves that way."

"I agree," said Jim.

"Me, too," added Pete. Other members of the crews nodded their heads or said that they agreed.

Frank stood up. "Then we should be able to handle complaints like these within the building," he continued, "rather than going to central office. Follow what I'm saying? We can't run a school without custodians, but we should be able to work without outside influences. If you have any problems, talk to me first." Frank sat down. Jim was shuffling his feet nervously in the second row.

Pete asked whether anyone had anything to add. No one said anything.

Frank stood up again. "Thank you all for letting me talk to you. By the way, I would like the gym to look sharp on Friday. We will have guests in the building."

Crew members from both shifts nodded, stood, and began to leave the room.

Frank hoped he had made his point. He wished Pete were tougher with the group, but he knew it was hard for Pete to be tough and work with these people at the same time. Still, he didn't want any more directives from McIsaac or central office.

CASE 3.7: MEETING OF THE DEPARTMENT HEADS

As Sharon walked into the room, she hoped that this meeting would not be long and tedious. She had a discussion to prepare for the American Novel class the next day, and she had barely begun to read that week's compositions from the sophomores. She was the last department head to arrive, and, as usual, all the men were seated at the right side of the table and all the women to the left. Dr. Meier, the principal, was seated in the middle between the two groups, and the assistant principal, Joe Bronson, was standing across the table from Dr. Meier. Though there were a couple of seats left next to the women, Sharon instead chose the one open seat next to Dr. Meier on the men's side of the table.

Mr. Bronson did not ever call the meeting to order but rather he quietly said, "Well, um, let's begin now." Mr. Bronson tried to describe the testing schedule that would be in effect during the final week of the semester, but Dr. Meier interjected more explanation three different times.

Copies of the agenda for the meeting were scattered around on the table. Mr. Bronson looked over at one of them and began to explain the first item, concerning a local speakers' bureau. He began to read from a brochure about the bureau, stumbling over several words. Sharon grimaced inside and tried to keep her feelings from showing on her face. Mr. Bronson said, "Now this person, he's a, a professor of pharmacy, I think."

"No," Dr. Meier said, "exercise physiology."

"Oh, yes," said Mr. Bronson with a giggle. Sharon always thought it strange that such a large man would giggle, but Mr. Bronson giggled often. "Well, he has a lot of program ideas you would be interested in, and you can use these programs."

"Do we work through you on this, or do we make the contacts ourselves?" Ethel Jones, business department head, asked.

"Well," Bronson responded, "I guess you could call him, but let me know, too."

"No," Dr. Meier interrupted, "we'll work through Mr. Bronson on these arrangements."

"Really," Sharon thought, "it's almost embarrassing. Mr. Bronson's job is to chair these meetings. But Dr. Meier always has to help him out. Bronson may have the position, but it's clear that Meier has the power."

Sharon was relieved when Mr. Bronson finally said, "Well, that covers everything, I think."

She started to leave when Dr. Meier responded, "Actually, I have several items to discuss." Sharon settled back in her chair as part two of the meeting began.

CASE 3.8: IGNORING
THE TEACHERS' RECOMMENDATIONS

Laura was fed up. She knew that Mrs. Crofton, her principal, trusted her judgment. After all, she had appointed Laura as head teacher, which meant she was in charge of the building when Mrs. Crofton was gone. She also knew she had the respect of other teachers. That was why they asked her to attend all of these Student Assistance Team meetings. She was convinced that the school district was taking the right approach in its policy requiring teachers and administrators to meet about students who were having academic or behavioral problems. If she knew all of these things, why couldn't she convince Mrs. Crofton that what the Student Assistance Teams recommended had to be taken seriously?

Mrs. Crofton had been opposed to the teams from the beginning. Though Mrs. Crofton never told the other teachers that she thought the teams were a bad idea, she told Laura that teachers could meet if they wanted to but that she didn't plan to meet with them. And Mrs. Crofton hadn't. When individual teachers or the school psychologist or the student's case worker requested a meeting, Mrs. Crofton arranged a place for the meeting but always managed to have another commitment.

The last team meeting had left teachers particularly angry about Mrs. Crofton's refusal to work with them. The student, Donald Baxter, was an especially difficult case. He had been recommended for special services by his second-, third-, and fourth-grade teachers, but he never tested low enough to qualify for any of the programs. While his academic performance was never more than marginal, his teachers were convinced that his biggest problem was immaturity. Now in fifth grade, Donald was frequently a problem in the halls, the rest rooms, and school assemblies. That was why the team had recommended that a behavior contract be developed for Donald. The team had also recommended that Mrs. Crofton be asked to begin the process.

When Jennifer Langrock, Donald's teacher who had asked for the team meeting, met with Mrs. Crofton to discuss the team's recommendation, Mrs. Crofton's response had been, "That's not what Donald needs." She had terminated the conference abruptly, saying she had another commitment, and neither Jennifer nor anyone else heard any more about Donald from Mrs. Crofton.

Jennifer had been livid. She went from Mrs. Crofton's office to the teachers' lounge, where she described the incident to anyone who would listen. And now Jennifer had requested Laura's help in convincing Mrs. Crofton. Laura just wasn't sure what she could or should do. After all, Donald wasn't Laura's student, and Mrs. Crofton wasn't her problem either.

CASE 3.9: CHAIRING THE AWARDS COMMITTEE

Jeannette had been lead teacher at Spring Hill Elementary School for over a year now, and here she was once again faced with chairing a committee of teachers and unsure of exactly what the principal, Mrs. Angotti, wanted the committee to do. The issue they were to consider was clear enough: How would the all-school awards assemblies be handled this year? What Jeannette didn't know was whether Mrs. Angotti expected the committee to make the decisions, or whether the committee was simply to give her advice about the awards and the program.

The committee met for the first time in October. Jeannette was relieved that none of those staff members who felt they had all the answers to everyone's questions had volunteered for the committee. Instead, the committee members included Susan Wilson, a paraprofessional in the language arts program and a hard worker who could be counted on; Phyllis Jacobson, a first-grade teacher who had been a member of the previous year's committee; Richard Moreno, a second-grade teacher who always had good ideas; and Donna Rauch, one of the special education teachers in the building.

Unfortunately, only Phyllis was in school on the day the first meeting was scheduled. It was easy enough for Jeannette and Phyllis to agree that only attendance awards would be given at the end of each quarter and that all other awards would be presented at the end of each semester. They also decided that awards for perfect attendance should be issued only to those students who were neither absent nor late in a quarter.

When Jeannette explained the recommendations that the committee had developed so far to Mrs. Angotti, she generally agreed with what had been decided except that she felt that being late for school should not be counted in granting the attendance awards. "We want our children to be in school," she said, "even if they are sometimes late." Jeannette was disappointed. She and Phyllis had thought that their guidelines would provide more incentive for students to be on time.

The committee met several more times before the end of the first semester to discuss how many assemblies there should be each year, what awards should be given at the all-school assemblies, what the awards should be, and what the program for the assemblies should be. Committee members decided that one assembly a year was too few, that awards should be presented at the end of each semester. They also agreed that awards should be given only for significant reasons. The "best smile" award at last year's assembly would not be repeated, even if that meant that some children at Spring Hill would not get an award. Awards for academic achievement would be given. In addition, awards would be presented for good citizenship and safe behavior on the school buses. The committee then decided to give an award to every student for "making the first semester so successful." The committee also decided that the ceremonies should be short, should be held in front of all the children, and should recognize each award winner individually.

At the final meeting of the committee in early January, all of these decisions were approved for presentation to Mrs. Angotti. When Jeannette met with Mrs. Angotti a week later, she was relieved to discover that Mrs. Angotti accepted the committee's recommendations without change. Mrs Angotti thanked her for her work as chair of the committee and told her she would send notes to all the committee members thanking them for their good ideas.

Later, Jeannette wondered why her only reaction afterwards was relief that the job had gone so smoothly. All of the committee's recommendations had been accepted by Mrs. Angotti except for the qualifications for attendance awards. While she was glad that the committee had come up with recommendations that were going to be used, she really hadn't been at all confident that Mrs. Angotti would agree with the committee until the committee's work was completed and the recommendations presented. She also was not sure how much the committee had kept in mind Mrs. Angotti's personal preferences while they developed the recommendations. Had they come up with the ideas that they felt were the best ones for the school and the children, or had they come up with ideas that they felt they could sell to Mrs. Angotti? If this is what chairing a committee is all about, Jeannette wasn't sure she wanted much to do with it. Shouldn't she feel better after having done a good job?

CASE 3.10: DISCIPLINING THE DEBATE TEAM

Jeff Benson, chair of the Speech Department, couldn't really get a sense of the problem yet, but he knew enough to understand that he had a very scared department member on his hands. Mark Steiner, seated across the table from him in the department office area, was shaking so much that his coffee was spilling over the edge of his mug.

"Okay, Mark," Jeff said, "tell me again what happened on your debate trip this weekend."

"Well," Mark began, "I don't really know how much of this matters, but this was only our second overnight trip of the year. I didn't have any problems at all with the team on the first trip. Maybe it was because I'm so new at West High, but this past weekend was a different story. They were rowdy from the time we left for the weekend. Several of the kids said things to each other and to me that I thought were rude, they were loud in the restaurant when we went out for supper, and then they were up most of Friday night before the debate rounds on Saturday. I finally went to the room where the four junior boys were staying. The rest of the team was there, with a few students from other schools. I told everyone that I wanted them in their own rooms, asleep, within ten minutes. Debbie Mackey told me to 'lighten up' and 'quit being an old fart' when I said that. I ignored her, but it really made me angry. Then Saturday they were tired, didn't debate well, and weren't any easier to get along with. We lost, of course. Didn't even make the quarter finals. And Debbie was the worst of the group. She's had a lousy attitude since the beginning of the year."

Jeff didn't know Debbie Mackey well. He knew who she was, of course. Everyone in school knew who Debbie was: tall, long blond hair, usually wore tight jeans, and had an arrogant sexy look. Jeff knew from other teachers that she was bright but difficult to deal with, just the sort of student likely to give a young, single, male teacher a hard time. "I'm really sorry to hear that, Mark. From everything I've heard from parents and students, you've done good work with the team so far. The students seem to like and respect you, and the parents appreciate the way you've kept them informed."

"Well, they're sure to change their minds about that now. You know, I tried to talk to Debbie about it on Monday. She refused to talk, ignored me when I tried to get her attention in the hallway before my speech class, didn't respond to the message I sent asking her to stop by my room after school. By Monday night I was really angry. She had not only spoiled the weekend for me and the team, but now she was refusing to talk about it. So I wrote her a letter—on legal paper, of course. How else would a debate coach write it? It was pretty long, four or five pages, and I was pretty frank. I don't have a copy of it; I didn't make one. But I know I said things like 'You don't give a fuck about the team,' and I know I used the word 'bitch' once or twice. As I said, I was pretty angry."

"Did you give the letter to Debbie?"

"Not exactly. By that time it was pretty late, about ten o'clock. I knew she works at the Burger Basket on Monday nights, but by the time I got there, she had already left. So I gave the letter to her boyfriend and asked him to give it to her. You don't know how much I wish now that I had just gone home and torn the damn thing up."

"So how did the principal become involved?"

"I didn't have any trouble sleeping Monday night. It had been a long weekend, and I'd had a couple of beers while I was writing the letter. But when I woke up Tuesday morning, I knew I had done absolutely the wrong thing. So I stopped by the principal's office and asked his secretary for an appointment to see him that day. I told her that Dr. Lyman might want to ask the senior girls' counselor to sit in, too, because it concerned one of the senior debaters."

"Did you tell Dr. Lyman the whole story?"

"Pretty much just as I've told it to you. Mary Cannon was there too, as I had suggested. Neither one of them seemed particularly upset by what I said. I told them that I had done a stupid thing, that they might be hearing about it. Dr. Lyman's reaction was, 'Let's just see what develops.'"

"And now, I take it, something has developed." Jeff really didn't want to put Mark through this, but he couldn't even begin to help if he didn't know the whole story.

"Mr. and Mrs. Mackey called Dr. Lyman Tuesday evening. They also called Superintendent Morrison. You know, Debbie's best friend is Brenda Morrison. No one called me. The next thing I knew, Dr. Lyman was standing in my room last period telling me to clear out my desk and that I've been suspended without pay. I don't know what to do, Jeff."

"Well, you can't deny that you wrote the letter."

"No," Mark replied, "but I'm a good teacher. I made a mistake. I need this job, and I won't resign."

Case 3.10: Part Two

Three weeks later Jeff still wasn't sure what had happened to Mark Steiner. There had been an administrative hearing the week after Jeff and Mark had talked. Jeff had done what he could to help out. He had submitted a written statement. In it he said that although a few of the debaters seemed to have trouble getting along with Mark, most of them had seemed to like and respect him. He described the long hours that Mark spent working with the team, and he described Mark as sincere, considerate, and a conscientious teacher. He noted that Mark's recommendations from his previous school had been very positive, and he said that in the one observation of Mark's teaching that he had conducted before the time of the incident, he had found Mark to be well prepared for class, insightful in his questioning of students and in his responses to their questions, and able to generate an enthusiasm in his students that was admirable. There was not much else he could say. He knew that some of the debaters and their parents had written letters to Dr. Lyman asking that Mark be reinstated.

He also knew that Mark was gone. Jeff wasn't sure of the details, but

Mark had stopped in to tell him that he had decided to resign at the superintendent's insistence. He also said the superintendent had offered to pay his salary for the rest of the semester and to provide him with a letter of reference that made no mention of the resignation if he would agree to stop teaching immediately. In light of their previous conversations, Jeff wasn't sure why Mark had decided to accept the terms. He wondered if Jeff realized how difficult it would be for him to find another teaching job if his credentials showed that he had taught at West only one semester. He also had the feeling that Mark thought Jeff hadn't done enough as department chair to support his case.

Case 3.10: Part Three

Dr. Lyman lost no time in replacing Mark, and the person selected to replace him raised some questions that concerned Jeff. The debate team had been scheduled to take another trip the weekend after the incident, but when Mark was suspended, the trip was cancelled. The organizer for that tournament was Brad Ellis, now the debate coach in a neighboring town, but Brad had been the coach at West High School prior to Mark's arrival. Jeff knew through the grapevine that Ellis had been sorry he made the change before he even took over in the new school. His family was still living in the West High district, and Jeff knew that Ellis had asked a couple of teachers about possible openings within the first two weeks of the new school year.

Jeff had heard from one of the assistant principals that Ellis had called Dr. Lyman on Monday or Tuesday after the cancellation and had been in for a job interview by the end of the week. Shortly after the interview, Jeff was told that Ellis would be reporting as a long-term substitute on Monday of the next week and that he would be employed in this capacity for the rest of the school year.

One of Jeff's concerns was that he hadn't been involved in hiring Ellis. Another concern was that the whole incident seemed suspect. Jeff had asked Lyman whether Ellis wasn't under contract with another district, but he had stopped short of suggesting that it seemed unethical to employ someone under contract with another district to fill a position that wasn't really vacant.

Lyman assured him that he had consulted with Superintendent Morrison and that Morrison had given his endorsement. Jeff felt that there was nothing more he could say. As he walked back to the department office, he thought about the unanswered questions. Why was Ellis's school district willing to let him go on such short notice? How did the guy know there was a vacancy at West High so soon after Mark's suspension? How could

Lyman get by with hiring his old friend Ellis when Ellis was under contract? And why was all this done without consultation with him, the department chair?

Mark shouldn't have written that letter, of course, but it had all worked out too conveniently for Dr. Lyman and Ellis. Jeff had a strong suspicion that the unfortunate incident with Mark had been used as a convenient way to get Ellis back to the district.

CASE 3.11: EVALUATING THE COACHES

Oak Grove was a small town and, as in many small towns, the school district sports program was of interest to many community members. Oak Grove Consolidated Schools had a long tradition of winning, especially in football and boys' basketball, though recently the girls' teams had done well in state competition and the boys' teams were in a slump.

Parent complaints about the program had increased during the past year. There were always parents who complained, of course. In fact, complaints as recently as five years earlier had resulted in a major change in school district policy about sports. The board approved a requirement that every coach play every team member in every game. While that policy had been accepted without question when the boys' teams were winning, recent losses had sometimes been blamed on the policy. Some parents of star players, in fact, had complained that their sons or daughters were not getting the playing time they deserved.

Superintendent of Schools Fritz Benson was well aware of the complaints. He always felt a bit uncomfortable when he had to deal with sports in the district. Because of his own lack of experience in coaching, and the limited experience of the elementary school principal, Jack Baker, and the secondary school principal, Dennis Luber, he had recommended several years before that the three administrators in the district (himself, Baker, and Luber) jointly assume the position of athletic director when the former athletic director retired. Though he knew the arrangement was unusual, he had justified it as an effort to highlight athletics as an integral part of the school program. Coaches would report to the principals and the superintendent as would any other instructional program. And he had to say that the arrangement had worked well. He and the principals generally agreed, and they had been able to handle the athletic responsibilities as part of their regular administrative meetings.

At a recent administrative meeting, Fritz had brought up complaints about the athletic program. "The problem," Jack said, "is that we really don't know what coaches are doing with those teams or what effects the athletic program is having on students."

"That's part of the problem," Dennis agreed, "though I wish I knew more about coaching. My seven years of assisting with Little League teams hasn't been much help."

"Maybe we need to check our data," Fritz suggested. "It could be that we are overly concerned about the complaints of a small group of parents. We should have a better sense of what the athletes and the parents really think."

It was then that he, Dennis, and Jack came up with the idea of asking parents and students to evaluate the athletic programs in Oak Grove. Dennis drafted a questionnaire. They went over it together at the next administrators' meeting and agreed on the format and questions (see below).

PARENT EVALUATION FORM: BOYS' BASKETBALL

I. Indicate the degree to which you agree with the following statements by circling a number:

	Very much	Somewhat	Not at all
a. My son enjoyed the sport.	1	2 3	4 5
b. My son learned the fundamentals of the sport.	1	2 3	4 5
c. My son's self-confidence improved.	1	2 3	4 5
d. My son's physical condition improved.	1	2 3	4 5
e. My son has learned sportsmanlike behavior.	1	2 3	4 5

II. Please rate the coaches on the following items. Use the following rating scale:
   1 = Excellent; 2 = Good; 3 = So-So; 4 = Weak; 5 = Poor; 6 = Don't Know.

	Coach Barta	Coach Watson
a. Treated my son fairly	———	———
b. Kept winning in perspective	———	———
c. Took safety precautions	———	———
d. Organized practice and contests	———	———
e. Communicated with me	———	———
f. Was effective in teaching skills	———	———

III. Please given any additional comments in the space below and on the back. Perhaps you have some constructive criticism or praise you want to offer.

They spent part of another meeting discussing how they would present this plan to the coaches.

As they discussed how to implement the evaluation, all three of them were very aware that Oak Grove had an unfortunate history of controversy about evaluation of teachers. During Fritz's ten years as superintendent, several grievances had been filed, and three teachers had threatened to file a civil suit against the principal who preceded Jack. Most of the bugs in the evaluation system had been worked out over time, but teachers were still skittish about the process.

Jack suggested that Fritz meet with the coaches individually and ask for their support. Fritz suggested building-level meetings. Dennis suggested drafting a letter to all coaches that included a copy of the questionnaire. They finally decided that all three of them would present the plan at a meeting for all coaches. That, they decided, would show that there was solidarity among them, that they had given the matter careful consideration, and that, although they were willing to listen to coaches' concerns, they were in agreement that some evaluation of the athletic program was needed. The meeting was set for the next Thursday at 7:30 A.M., the only time when all coaches were available.

Case 3.11: Part Two

None of them was prepared for the intensity of the coaches' reactions when the evaluation plan was described to them. They hadn't expected the coaches to be enthusiastic, but neither had they expected the misunderstanding and distrust that was evident at the meeting. Jack had begun the meeting by reporting that the administrative team had decided to use parents and athletes in the evaluation of the coaching staffs and their programs at the end of each sport season. As Jack continued to describe the plan, coaches began voicing their opposition. When it became clear that there was little support for the proposal, Fritz said, "There will be some form of parent involvement in the evaluation." As coaches continued to object, Dennis tried to meet what he thought was their main objection. "You are all taking it for granted," he said, "that the results will be negative. I believe that the evaluations will be good, for the most part."

Jerry Danby, the baseball coach, was the most vocal in his objections. He asked several questions about the validity and legality of the process the administrators had proposed. When it was clear that nothing would be resolved that day, Fritz suggested that a committee be formed to consider the best way to implement the program. Several coaches volunteered, including Danby.

Though the committee had not yet met, the coaches had evidently been meeting on their own. Now Jerry Danby was in Fritz's office as appointed spokesperson for the coaches. The coaches, Danby reported, were upset and offended by the show of power that the administration had demonstrated at the Thursday meeting. Several felt that the proposed coaches' evaluation was one more example of the superintendent's continuing attempts to discredit teachers by giving unwarranted attention to parents' opinions. Danby reported that there were rumors among the teachers that similar evaluations were planned for the vocal and instrumental music programs and for the drama program and the newspaper. Two of the coaches had contacted the state high school athletic association to ask about the legality of the evaluation plan. They had learned, Danby reported, that while the plan was legal, it was highly unusual and could be viewed as singling coaches out for special scrutiny. None of the coaches, Danby concluded, supported the plan. Moreover, he didn't think that anything or anyone could change their minds.

Fritz thanked Danby for serving as spokesperson for the coaches concerns and made a note to discuss the evaluation at the administrative team meeting that week.

Case 3.11: Part Three

Two months later the evaluation system was in place and Fritz wasn't sure what he had gained. The coaches' committee had met. They had recommended that parent and student evaluations be used as only one kind of data in evaluating the athletic programs. Though that was what the administrators had intended all along, Fritz had thanked the committee for their help and sent out the evaluation forms for the winter sports.

Responses had not been good. Forms had been returned by only half of the parents of the boys' basketball team, and there were even fewer responses from the parents of wrestlers. The responses from disgruntled parents were predictable, but only a few parents indicated strong satisfaction with the program. Athletes had filled out the forms because the coaches had distributed them at the last team meetings of the season, but the kids had obviously not given much thought to their answers.

The coaches were still upset by the process. They were obviously anxious to see the results when the forms were returned, and the structure of the form, which provided for evaluation of both the coach and the assistant coach on the same form, had led to some unfortunate comparisons of performance. The rumors about expanding the evaluation system to other extracurricular programs had not died down, in spite of frequent denials of any such intent on the part of the administrators.

Now it was time to evaluate the spring sports. Fritz wasn't sure what to do, and he was convinced that the other two members of the administrative team were at least as confused as he was.

CASE 3.12: SHE WAS A GOOD TEACHER FOR 25 YEARS

"This wouldn't be nearly so tough," Fred thought, "if it were anyone but Martha Trauner. The woman has given 1,000 percent in her work with kids all the years I've known her . . . until now. And now she just doesn't seem able to do it."

Pete Hanson, the seventh-grade science teacher, had just left Fred's office after reporting Martha had been late for work once again that morning. Fred knew Pete was telling the truth when he said he hated to say anything but that Martha had been late several times in the previous couple of months and the students in her first-hour class were getting out of hand and disturbing other classes in the wing. Pete had been delegated by the other teachers in the wing to talk to Fred, but he was also disturbed himself. In fact, he said, he was worried about Martha.

Fred knew that Martha's life hadn't been easy in the past couple of years. First, her husband had died unexpectedly. Then her middle son had been in some kind of trouble with drugs. And one daughter had gone through a nasty divorce and come home to live with Martha for a while. Still, other people had troubles too. Martha's problems had seemed to force her deeper and deeper into herself.

When Fred first became principal at Hollings Junior High School, Martha was clearly one of the finest teachers he had ever met. She worked well with students. Her lessons were well prepared, and her enthusiasm about literature and art was contagious. She got students excited about learning.

The complaints had started early the previous school year. Martha began having trouble handling a few students, and she seemed distracted much of the time. A few parents complained about inconsistent grading or assignments that weren't clearly defined. Two families asked to have their children transferred to other classes. Teachers who had always been Martha's friends seemed to avoid her, and Fred had heard rumors that she had started drinking heavily. He had tried to talk to her about it at the end of the year, but Martha became very defensive. "Fred," she said, "I've been a fine teacher for 25 years. Don't you trust me anymore? I'm tired; just give me the summer to rest up."

But the summer hadn't seemed to help. In fact, the problems were more serious this year. Pete wasn't the first staff member who had complained about Martha. Martha often looked tired and disheveled. She had little patience with her students, and Fred had heard her yelling to get the attention of a class more than once as he had wandered around the building. He had observed her teach once since the school year began, and though he couldn't see any serious problems during his observation, neither she nor the students showed any of the enthusiasm that had distinguished Martha's teaching before. And when Fred tried to talk to her about this change, she simply asked him what she needed to do to satisfy him. That wasn't at all like the Martha he used to know, the one who would have been more concerned with satisfying herself. And being late was not something he could ignore. He would talk to her within the next day.

Case 3.12: Part Two

Fred's conference with Martha had not gone well. He was prepared with the facts as he had learned them through a few discreet questions to other teachers in Martha's wing of the building. Martha had been late at least twice a week during the past month or so, often as much as ten minutes for her first class. Within the past two days, three parents had called with complaints. One said he had left messages for Martha on two different occasions and she had failed to return his calls. Martha's first-quarter grades had been turned in late, and the teacher who substituted for her the previous week had filed a very uncomplimentary report.

Martha had denied everything. She denied ever hearing from the parent who said she did not return his calls, and she said that the only problems she had were with children who were too rude and undisciplined to be in school. The substitute teacher had misunderstood her directions and believed everything the children had said to fool her. Martha did admit that she had been late, but only a couple of times and only because of car problems that she couldn't help. She assured him it wouldn't happen again.

When Fred asked if she had considered working with a counselor to help her deal with some of her personal problems, Martha had become very angry. "Listen, Fred," she said, "you're a principal, not a psychiatrist. My personal problems are just that, personal. If you have any complaints about my job, let me know. If you're worried about my personal life, don't waste your time."

When Martha walked out of his office, Fred knew that he had a serious problem on his hands.

Case 3.12: Part Three

Fred wasn't quite sure why his conversation with Russell Patterson, the director of personnel, left him feeling so uncomfortable. Russell had pretty much described the options he already knew. First, there was the Employee Assistance Program. Martha could get time off for counseling if she wanted it. Second, there was suspension with or without pay. If her personal problems were having serious and documentable effects on her work with students, she could be forced to get help. Finally, there was termination, but Russ had warned him that it would be a lengthy and difficult process, particularly difficult if he attempted to do it before the end of the school year. If his own attempts to talk to Martha about her problems were any indication, she was unlikely to go along with the counseling. The other two options seemed like terrible things to do to a dedicated teacher who was obviously in trouble.

Fred decided he had to make one more attempt to get Martha to admit to her own problems, and he decided he was willing to take some risks to do that. He talked at some length to Phyllis Jefferson and Annette Wilkins, staff members who were about Martha's age who had once been her friends. Both of them had virtually given up trying to help Martha, but both agreed to make one more attempt. He also enlisted the help of Jack Zerlin, one of the school counselors who had worked for several years as a volunteer with Alcoholics Anonymous. He invited all of them—Martha, Phyllis, Annette, and Jack—to a Saturday morning meeting at his lake house, ostensibly to discuss a new cross-age program in humanities for junior high students. Martha had said she would be there, although she had seemed surprised when he asked her. Jack arranged to have an A. A. counselor there as well.

Fred almost lost his nerve the morning of the meeting. After everyone had arrived and coffee and doughnuts were served, Fred told Martha that the reason they were all there was to help her, to show her that they were concerned, and to give her their support. Martha threatened to leave, but Phyllis told her that she would have to walk; Phyllis had hidden her car keys. Martha denied that she had problems, but every one had come with evidence of problems in the past two years. Martha had cried, yelled, paced, but finally broke down and said, "What do you want me to do?" The A. A. counselor was prepared with a whole list of things she could do, beginning with admitting she had a problem. Martha had finally agreed to seek help. The session ended in more tears than Fred felt comfortable with, but he thought he had done what he had to do.

Case 3.12: Postscript

A year later Fred was no longer sure about what was right. In many ways, Martha's was a success story. It hadn't been easy. She had tried counseling, then quit. Fred finally told her that it was counseling or her job. She eventually requested a leave of absence for the remainder of the school year, received treatment for her alcohol problems, and put her life back together.

In the fall she returned to the classroom. Now, three weeks into the new school year, he had four letters from parents requesting that their children be transferred to a "more qualified" teacher. One even used the word "wino" in describing Martha. What's more, several of the teachers seemed vindictive. They avoided Martha whenever possible, and one had requested a change of duty when assigned to supervise a study hall with her. He noticed that many of them ignored her, and he often saw her sitting by herself in the teachers' room or eating her lunch in her room. She was a good teacher; she was proving that already in her work with her classes. But Fred wasn't sure that others were willing to give her a chance.

CHAPTER 4

Managing Program Design and Delivery

I can think of nothing so sorely missing in the teaching profession as the engagement of teachers in contemplating what schools should be, what children should learn, and what teaching might become. Schools badly need inhabitants who ask why . . . .

Roland Barth

CASE 4.1: DEVELOPING THE NINTH-GRADE STUDY CENTER

Willis Cochran, principal of Willa Cather High School, frequently walked the halls of the school while classes were in session. He had been convinced of the values of "management by wandering around" long before the notion became popularized in the management literature. Usually he just moved around the building, almost at random. Some days, such as today, he had a particular mission: He was interested in the progress of the ninth-grade study center, a phenomenon new to Willa Cather High with the addition of a ninth grade this past fall. It struck him as ironic that the two students he met on his way to the study center were ninth graders of dubious reputations, who told him they were headed for the Social Studies Instructional Materials Center to work on a class assignment and showed him their passes.

Passes also were a new phenomenon at Willa Cather High School. The school functioned on a modular schedule, with students in grades ten, eleven, and twelve free to move about the building—or outside of the building—with no supervision by faculty or administration. In the 15 years that Willa Cather had been operating on a modular schedule, there had been very few students who were unable to take responsibility for their own behavior. Cochran credited the staff for the success of the program. Faculty were careful to assign work to students that required their use of the instructional materials centers, set high expectations for student performance, and provided support for those students who seemed unable to work within the system.

The shift of ninth graders from the junior high schools to the high school introduced a new problem. Parents of eighth graders indicated in a survey conducted during the previous school year that they were concerned about the lack of structure at the high school and that they felt their children would need more direction. The school district had responded by scheduling more classes for ninth graders and by providing study centers for students when they did not have classes. Yet even with their heavier class schedules, ninth graders could have as many as three unscheduled mods a day.

Willis had been unsure about how to proceed with planning for the study centers. Fortunately, he gained another assistant principal with the shift of the ninth graders. Julian Capezio had been a junior high school principal, and Willis turned the problem of the study centers over to him. While Willis had pictured a traditional study hall with quiet students and strict discipline, Julian had other ideas. Two teachers and two aides had been assigned to the study centers, and Julian worked with them to develop a program for the incoming ninth-grade students.

During the first week, ninth graders were given introductions to each academic department's instructional materials center. Study skills were incorporated into each day's presentation. Every student assigned to study centers went through this curriculum. After the first week, Julian had introduced a pass system so that students could sign out of the study centers and into the instructional materials centers. Julian made sure that every ninth-grade teacher was assigning work outside of class and encouraging students to use the centers.

Julian and his study center staff met every Friday morning during the first few weeks of school to discuss problems, and they continually revised the program for the study centers. By group decision, they permitted students to sit together and converse in the cafeteria. In the afternoons particularly, the cafeteria was frequently chaotic. Though a teacher or an aide supervised the area, Willis had never seen a student reprimanded for talking too much or too loudly. The aides and teachers tolerated a great deal more than Willis would have, and that leniency made him very uncomfortable.

At the same time, Willis had to recognize the success of the approach that Julian and his staff had taken. Teachers, who were blissfully unaware of the chaos Willis saw in the cafeteria, had few complaints about the ninth graders. The supervisors of the media centers had reported high use of the centers by the ninth-grade students. Just recently, only eight weeks into the school year, staff had been asked to rate ninth graders on their ability to handle responsibility. Julian intended those students who were rated as responsible by teachers, had their parents' permission, and had no history of discipline problems to be exempted from study centers at the beginning of the second nine-week grading period. Teachers' responses indicated that 65 percent of the ninth graders would no longer be assigned to supervised study. That was success by anyone's measure.

As Willis approached the cafeteria, he could hear the noise. It was two o'clock, and ninth graders seemed more interested in socializing than working on school assignments. The teacher on duty seemed unaware of any problem. He didn't even react when he noticed Willis standing at the side of the room.

Willis continued down the hall to the classroom assigned for supervised study, where Julian was on duty. He paused before he opened the door. "I'm not sure what I'm doing here," he thought. "I gave Julian a job to do, and he did it. He did it differently than I would have done it. He probably did it better. Why, then, do I have this nagging feeling that something is wrong and I have to do something to make it right?"

Without answering his own question, Willis opened the door and entered the room.

CASE 4.2: WOULD THIS BE GOOD FOR MY KIDS?

Clint Reeves, assistant superintendent for personnel in the Green Lake School District, was never one for small talk. He began the business of their meeting as soon as Raphael (Ray) Hernandez, principal at Pine View Elementary School, entered the room.

"Thanks for coming in, Ray. I'm interested in getting the principals' personnel recommendations as early as possible this spring."

"No problem. I appreciate the chance to talk about it with you."

"What are your recommendations?"

"As you will recall, we've had one first-year teacher, Margaret Finch, and one second-year teacher, Kent Rawling, at Pine View this year. I've observed their teaching, as has the district's elementary supervisor, and I'm recommending that contracts be renewed for both of them."

"Very good."

"They're both strong teachers, Clint, fresh and energetic. Each of them has added something special to Pine View."

"Glad to hear that."

"I've saved the tough one for last: Martha Stoneham." Ray watched as Clint grimaced, then caught himself.

"You remember that we've talked about Martha several times this year."

"Yes, but review the situation for me, will you?"

"Be glad to. Martha joined the faculty at Pine View last September on a transfer from Cedar Ridge Elementary. She had received unfavorable teaching evaluations there over a two-year period, and the principal recommended that she be placed on probation. She joined my faculty as a teacher on probation with 30 years of teaching experience in the district. An unusual situation, to say the least."

"Ray, did you ever discuss Martha's work with the principal at Cedar Ridge?"

"No, I didn't. I'd heard rumors, of course, but I wanted to give her every benefit and to have as little history as possible."

"But you didn't find her work satisfactory?"

"No, it was difficult from the beginning. I started receiving complaints from parents during the first month of school. I think I must have called you about the situation in early October."

"I remember. You asked to end Martha's contract with the district at the semester. I couldn't support that, Ray. You can't take a loyal employee such as Martha and release her after 30 years of service, three years before she's scheduled to retire. Her husband had died. Her sons had recently moved away. She needed some time to recover from her losses."

"I could understand your position, Clint, so we tried. Fortunately, my faculty are real professionals. Over the year, I think each of them tried in some way to help. The supervisor spent a good deal of time with her. Finally we surrounded her with good teachers and worked around her."

"Martha loves kids."

"No doubt about that, but the children were missing a great deal of what children in other classes were getting. Martha is very traditional, and my faculty are committed to the district's individualized instructional model. Every time I observed Martha teach, I asked myself whether I would want my own children to be in her class. With this perspective, I could understand parents' complaints, and I found it hard to explain to them why their children were not having the same experiences as other fourth graders."

"What's your recommendation, Ray?"

"I recommend dismissal."

"I can't support that. Martha does not do harm to children. She's been with the district 30 years. She's two years from retirement. Ray, she taught the superintendent's children, and he thinks she's great. The most I could recommend is moving her to another school. I think Oak Hill will have a fourth-grade opening."

"I was afraid you'd say that, and I've thought about it a lot. If that's the best the district can do, I will keep Martha on my staff. I want you to know that I think the district is making a mistake here. All our statements about 'commitment to excellence' are meaningless unless they apply to *all* our teachers. But given the circumstances, I don't think another move is the answer. My staff have learned to work around Martha. We can continue to do that . . . for the good of the children."

"Thanks, Ray. I appreciate your help. The superintendent will appreciate it too."

Ray felt tired and depressed as he got up to leave. Sometimes he wondered whether he could make a difference, but he knew he would have to resign if he ever really believed his own doubts. Martha Stoneham would still be teaching in Green Lake School District. What, if anything, could he do to provide a better education for her students?

CASE 4.3: GETTING HELP FOR MARGARET

"Fran," Donna Atwood, the school psychologist began, "I know you feel very strongly that Margaret Fisher should have special education placement, but there's a problem."

"What's that?" Fran asked, looking up from the third-grade arithmetic papers that she had been correcting.

"She tests too low for resource services," Donna explained, "but she is not low enough for placement in one of the other special education programs."

Exasperation and fatigue were reflected in Fran's voice. "The child is having trouble doing third-grade work. She was having trouble last year with second-grade work. Are you telling me she is too far behind to get the kind of help she needs?"

"Yes," Donna replied, "I suppose you could say it that way, though by next year at this time she will probably be far enough behind her classmates to qualify for a different placement."

"And in the meantime?"

"Do what you've been doing," Donna suggested. "Help her when you can, work with the resources you have, wait it out. She's not a problem in class, is she?"

"No discipline problem." Fran sighed. "I just can't give her what she needs and still help the others. Thanks, Donna, I know you tried. The whole thing just seems crazy to me sometimes."

CASE 4.4: RACIAL BALANCE
IN THE MAGNET SCHOOL

Superintendent Don Bascom wasn't sure which were harder to deal with, the Green Willow School District's successes or its failures. Malcolm Shabazz Elementary Science Center was clearly one of the successes. This school year there had been 150 open slots in the fourth grade at Malcolm Shabazz, and the district had received applications for over 700 children. Now that was success!

"But nothing is ever that easy," Don thought. Now several influential members of the black community, including the two black members of the board of education, were proposing a change in the selection guidelines. When Malcolm Shabazz opened four years earlier after several million dollars were spent to renovate the building and equip it as a science magnet, the board had supported the idea on the condition that Malcolm Shabazz be a true magnet. It would attract white students into the black neighborhood where the school was located, and it would be equally accessible to all students in the district. By board policy, the racial balance at Malcolm Shabazz was to be the same as the racial balance in the school district, 30 percent black and 70 percent nonblack.

At the last meeting of the school board's committee on instruction, one of the black board members, Galvin Johnson, had laid out the arguments for a change in the racial balance guidelines. "Yes," Johnson had begun, "the purpose of a magnet is to attract white students for voluntary integration, but the school is located in a part of the city where the percentage of blacks is greater than the 30 percent guideline. We need to stop busing black children who want to go to a neighborhood school out of the neighborhood. We need to encourage our black children to study science, and that's what Malcolm Shabazz is all about."

Within three days after the committee meeting, Don learned that the parent association at Malcolm Shabazz was organizing a counterattack. He wasn't surprised, then, to receive this letter from "The Malcolm Shabazz Magnet Task Force" in the morning mail:

Dear Dr. Bascom:

Concerned parents and teachers at Malcolm Shabazz Elementary Science Center have formed a task force to act as representatives of the Shabazz community as the Board of Education considers possible changes in the racial balance guidelines for Malcolm Shabazz.

Let us make our position absolutely clear. As members of the Shabazz community, we affirm our commitments to the following:

- the importance of continuing to draw students from the entire school district;
- the importance of maintaining Malcolm Shabazz as a pure science magnet;
- the need for continuing financial investment in Malcolm Shabazz to maintain the quality of the program;
- our insistence that parents and faculty be included in any discussion of substantive changes in the program.

While we are willing to work with you and the Board of Education on any reasonable plan to improve the quality of education for children at Malcolm Shabazz, we are resolute in our support for the above principles.

We are ready to meet with you immediately—as soon as this Saturday morning—to discuss our concerns. Please let us know what we can do to maintain this premium program in Green Willow School District.

Sincerely,
Malcolm Shabazz Magnet Task Force

Don dialed the extension of Glenda Ridenour, the assistant superintendent for curriculum. When Glenda answered, he asked her if she had a few minutes to talk about the Malcolm Shabazz problem.

Glenda stopped in Don's office a few minutes later with a file of papers under her arm. "I've made a few phone calls," she began. "I knew you'd be interested in what other school districts have done about racial balance in their magnet schools. I've talked to people in Tulsa and in St. Paul. I'm waiting for several people to return my calls."

"What have you found out so far?"

"In Tulsa, which is about the size of Green Willow, the racial guideline for the magnet schools is 50 percent black and 50 percent white. In fact, the district representative I talked to in Tulsa said that guidelines were the only way the school district sold the plan to the black community there. St. Paul gives preference to students who live in the magnet school's attendance area. That means that magnet schools located in black neighborhoods are likely to have racial compositions more like their neighborhood than like the school district. But remember that St. Paul has several magnet schools—over 30, I think."

"I'm thinking we're going to have to move on this," Don replied. "The parents of the students now at Malcolm Shabazz won't like it, but it seems to me we're going to have to move to a 35 percent or even 40 percent guideline."

"You may be right," Glenda mused. "That would mean that a larger number of blacks could attend the neighborhood school rather than being bused to other areas. But are you ready to take on the white parents on this issue? The school district put a lot of money and attention into Malcolm Shabazz. What will the white parents do when they find out that their children can't take advantage of it?"

CASE 4.5: THE LIE ABOUT CLASS SIZE

"Susan, I probably shouldn't tell you this because I know you'll be upset," Janet began as Susan walked into the faculty workroom, "but you're the head teacher in this building. Besides, the whole thing involves you. Are you aware that Mrs. Johnson is not reporting the right number of students for your class?"

"What do you mean, she's not reporting the right number of students? I know she knows how many students I have because when she put two new fifth graders in my room last week, I told her 33 was too many for all of us. It's not just me, but every additional child means that it takes us longer to do simple things, that there are just more bodies in a crowded room, and that I have less time for those who really need help."

"Of course she knows how many you have. She also knows that the Personnel Department doesn't like principals to report class sizes over 30. So I think she just adds them to someone else's tally."

CASE 4.6: COORDINATING
THE SPECIAL EDUCATION CURRICULUM

Marlene Nelson knew that Harvey Wilson, supervisor of special education for the secondary level in Dawson Public Schools, didn't relish meeting with her and the other high school special education coordinators, but she wished that just once he would be on time. She glanced again at the wall clock: 3:10, and the meeting was supposed to start at 3:00. No one else seemed concerned. Representatives from several of the other buildings were helping themselves to cookies and punch and making small talk at the back of the room; a few others hadn't arrived yet. Marlene didn't want cookies, and she was in no mood for small talk. It was time to get on with this.

Harvey rushed into the room, pulling a small stack of papers from the portfolio he carried. He passed the papers out—copies of the agenda for the meeting—then took off his suit coat and sat at one side of the long table that nearly filled the room. Finally, at 3:20, all ten building representatives had arrived. Harvey attempted to begin the meeting: "Okay, let's go ahead and get started." No one seemed to pay much attention to him.

He tried again: "Well, let's go." And finally, "Okay, let's see if we can get some kind of order here; Sue, you're out of order." The building representatives finally found seats around the table and turned their attention to Harvey and his agenda.

Harvey began by reviewing the item referred to as "upcoming events" and asked the representatives if any of them had other announcements. He briefly described the current status of the district's new curriculum model, and he responded to questions about the involvement of the special education high school representatives in the development of the model, a topic that had been covered at the last meeting.

Marlene yawned mentally. "Nothing new again," she thought.

Just then, however, she saw Dave Jenkins, the representative from West High School, sit up straighter and stare at Pauline Crawley, the representative from Southeast High, who was explaining how she uses regular education courses and materials with her special education students. "It works," Pauline concluded, "and I think it's something we all should try. Students like using the same materials as the other students in their classes. We should use all the materials we can from the regular curriculum whenever . . . ."

"I disagree," Dave interrupted. "The regular classes are too difficult for special needs students, and the materials are inappropriate. These students wouldn't be placed in special education classes if they could handle the courses and materials in the regular classroom."

"I agree," added Marlys Novatny, the representative from Northeast High School. "Our program should be different, distinctly different from the regular curriculum."

Renee Bartee, the representative from South High, nearly rose up out of her chair as she responded. "We could use the same materials *if* they are appropriate given the student's individual educational plan and *if* we adapt them as appropriate. I don't really see anything to discuss. In fact, I wonder when the rest of the faculty is going to get smart and individualize as we do."

Each of the other representatives gave his or her opinion, some arguing that materials from the regular curriculum should be incorporated into the special education program whenever possible and some arguing that materials from the regular curriculum were absolutely to be avoided. Marlene kept herself out of it. She was curious, however, about how Harvey would handle this deviation from his agenda. So far he had done nothing. Emotions were flaring, and the discussion had escalated into a comparison of the programs at the various high schools and the abilities of the students and teachers. Once Harvey tried to speak, but he only got out "I'd like to say . . . " before the discussion continued without him. He tried again a few minutes later: "Well, I think basically . . . . " Again, his attempt went nowhere.

The discussion was winding down. Renee suggested that the special education coordinators needed to develop procedures for the introduction, discussion, and implementation of major curriculum changes. She reminded the group that they had discussed these issues at several other meetings, and each time there had been no results.

A few minutes later, Harvey made his third attempt to get control of the meeting. It worked this time, but only because he talked louder than anyone else and refused to be interrupted. "I think that while some special education students may benefit from courses in the regular curriculum, the special education curriculum should be distinct and different. We are all part of a large district; therefore, individual schools may differ. I want to thank all of you for sharing your opinions on this. Now let's move on to the next item, planning the job fair for special education students."

"Bless his heart," Marlene thought, "Harvey's done it again. He let a discussion go on forever, then ended it by stating his own opinion without really acknowledging the differences in the group. Two months from now when the issue comes up again, we will cover the same territory and still not reach any agreement." Meanwhile, Harvey had finished with the job fair and moved on to passing out the forms for textbook orders. Marlene checked off that item on her agenda and glanced at the clock just one more time.

CASE 4.7: IS IT TIME TO GIVE UP ON DENNIS?

Principal Gene Lehman was not surprised to see Dennis Wilson sitting in one of the chairs outside his office door. It seemed as though Dennis had been a regular in that spot during his two years at Woodruff Junior High School. Dennis held the standard referral form in his left hand; his right hand tapped out the rhythm to a song that only he was hearing. "Okay, Dennis," Gene began, "what's the problem today?"

"You can read it," Dennis said, handing Gene the referral form.

"Right," Gene replied, taking the form from him. "I'll be with you in a minute." He walked into his office, sat down at the desk, and looked at the report. It was from Ralph Douglas, one of the physical education teachers. Dennis, he said, had been found smoking a joint in the locker room during an activity period.

Gene reached behind him and opened the drawer that contained his personal notes on those Woodruff students who, like Dennis, were frequently in trouble. Gene didn't need much help from his notes here. His notes went back almost two years, to the first month Dennis had been at Woodruff as a seventh grader. He was a likable kid, lazy, sometimes sullen, but not especially tough or difficult for teachers to handle. His grades were very low, usually "D's" and "F's," and he had been suspended twice in two years, once for failing to spend time in detention after he skipped school and a second time almost a year later for writing a sexually explicit note to one of the girls in his social studies class. Teachers and Dennis's counselor had suspected drug use, but this was the first time that drugs had been an issue in school.

Use of marijuana on school property was grounds for expulsion under the school district's discipline policy. That was clear enough. "The tragedy," Gene thought, "is that school is just about the only thing that Dennis has."

Dennis lived with his mother, but Gene knew that the mother was not much support for Dennis. She had a long history of problems with drugs and alcohol herself, and she sometimes disappeared for two or three days at a time. Mrs. Wilson had been contacted by teachers, the counselor, the school psychologist, and Gene himself over the past two years, and she had brought Dennis back to school each time he was suspended. Placement in a foster home had been considered for Dennis, but Mrs. Wilson was absolutely opposed to the idea, and the child welfare office had been reluctant to proceed.

The file also contained Gene's notes documenting staff meetings about Dennis, adjustments in his academic program, efforts to get help for him through the Boys' Club and the local Catholic parish, the weight-lifting program that one of the coaches had tried. Nothing really seemed to take; Dennis had drifted through these efforts as he drifted through the school day—passive, sullen, quiet, unaffected.

"Someone is going to have to figure out something to do for this child," Gene thought. He looked out at Dennis, still tapping out the rhythm to his song. Gene pulled the expulsion form from his desk drawer and began the paperwork.

CASE 4.8: THE WEEKEND COURSE

"Dr. Chang? This is Michelle Lee-Phillips calling, the librarian at Sojourner Truth Elementary School. You might remember me from the award you presented at our school last spring on behalf of the superintendent."

"Yes, Michelle. What can I do for you?"

"I sent a request for approval to enroll in a university course to your office two weeks ago. I haven't received a reply, and I wondered if you have had a chance to look at it."

"Yes, I planned to call you. Did you talk about taking this course with your principal?"

"Mrs. Witherspoon and I discussed it briefly. When I told her the course was called 'Library Services for Exceptional Students,' she said she thought it sounded interesting."

"To be frank, Michelle, I have some reservations about the course. As I recall, Central State College is offering the course here in Oak Valley. Is it a graduate course?"

"The registration materials describe it as a three-credit workshop. I don't know whether that means it's a graduate course, but I think it is."

"When does the class meet, and what are the course requirements?"

"The class meets one weekend this fall—Friday night, all day Saturday, and Sunday morning. Students have to complete a project after the class is over."

"Michelle, I have some concerns about the quality of courses Central State is offering. Why are you taking this class instead of one offered by our local university?"

"Convenience, in part. It's easier for me to spend one whole weekend on a class than to have sessions every week at night for a whole semester. The tuition at Central State is cheaper. Besides, the courses at the university aren't always very practical, if you know what I mean. I know I'll be able to use the project I do for this course in my library."

"If I'm going to approve college credits for advancement on the salary schedule, I have to be assured that the credits are worthwhile. People I've talked to who have taken Central State courses joke about the lack of rigor."

"Well, I don't know about that, Dr. Chang. All I know is that this course sounds useful and interesting, and that's important to me."

"Let me think about it, Michelle, and do some checking. I promise I'll get a response to you by the end of the week."

Dr. Chang hung up the phone, paused, then dialed the number of an old friend, Professor Craig Donovan, chairman of the Department of Curriculum and Instruction at the local university.

"Hello, Professor Donovan, this is Kitty Chang."

"Great to hear from you, Kitty. How have you been?"

"Assistant superintendents are always busy, of course, but the new job is going well. I called because I have some questions about a media course that Central State College is offering in Oak Valley this fall."

"Kitty, I know just the class you mean. We talked about it during our department meeting the other day."

"How does Central State's course compare to courses in media that you offer?"

"Well, I don't like to bad-mouth the competition, but we couldn't offer that course. We are required to have a person holding a doctorate teach our graduate courses. Courses have to meet for a total of 45 hours in order to qualify as three-credit courses. Most of our graduate courses require at least one substantial paper and a final exam. I don't think Central State worries about any of those things."

"How can they offer courses the way they do?"

"They don't have anyone over there who oversees the quality of their courses, and they seem to have found a market here. Every class they've offered in Oak Valley has filled easily, I'm told."

"I don't know what to do. One teacher has already asked for permission to take the course for advancement on the salary schedule. I'm sure there will be others."

"I'm sure there will be, Kitty. I can't tell you what to do. I only know that we can't stop Central State from offering courses such as the media course. The school districts are in a much better position to do that than the university."

"What do you mean?"

"Kitty, they couldn't offer the courses if teachers didn't sign up for them. Teachers wouldn't sign up for them if school districts refused to approve them."

"I see what you mean. Thanks for the information. Let's have lunch sometime soon and catch up with each other."

"I'd enjoy it. Then you can tell me what you decided to do about Central State."

CASE 4.9: THE ENGLISH CURRICULUM AT MEMORIAL

Joye McClune, the new assistant principal at Memorial Senior High School, was always a bit amazed when she visited the English Department office area. Because the department had no storage space and department members taught in several different classrooms, the office area included a desk for each faculty member and all the books that were used in the English curriculum. Joye felt as if she were visiting old friends as she walked through the area: *Huckleberry Finn*, *Silas Marner*, *The Turn of the Screw*, *The Outsiders*.

"Ah, the books," Joye thought, "they are wonderful, and they are the problem."

Joye had worked at Memorial High for only six months. When she had first arrived, a transfer from another city high school, she soon learned that the English Department was considered one of the strongest departments at Memorial. Bill Kenniston, the chair of the department, had been at the school 20 years. Though he was not a strong leader in conventional ways, he was a grandfatherly, scholarly person, an old-fashioned English teacher who loved books and jazz and children who liked to read. He had built the program, and he had built it with books.

Early in the fall, Joye had spent a few hours with Bill talking about his plans for the department. He said that the faculty agreed that some of the elective courses at the junior level needed to be revised. Joye soon understood that revising the courses meant nothing more than changing some of the books, adding some titles to one course and moving some titles between two other courses.

Joye had asked whether students were able to use word processing software and whether there was a sequence of experiences in oral communication in the curriculum. Bill's answers had been disconcerting. The department had only two computers, one of which was shared with the custodial crew, who kept it in their office. Even more alarming was Bill's report that most of the faculty did not see a place for computers in the English curriculum. While Bill assured Joye that the course requirements met the district's stipulations for written composition, faculty didn't feel they needed computers to do so. Bill also said that he knew that a few faculty members required students to give speeches but that no one saw a need for more emphasis on oral communication in the program. Their students, he said, seemed very adept at oral language, especially in the halls, cafeteria, and study rooms.

In other words, Joye concluded, members of the English department were satisfied with their program and didn't acknowledge the lack of balance that she saw in the program.

Joye hadn't pushed the issues, knowing that she needed some time to become familiar with the school and to let the faculty get to know her. She did take time in the next few months to visit classes. She watched Fran Worsinski, for example, teach *The Martian Chronicles* to tenth graders. Fran relied heavily on worksheets that required students to answer very specific questions about plot development and characters. Reading assignments were short, usually less than ten pages. She knew it took Fran nearly a month to finish *The Martian Chronicles* with her classes. Gary Brittan told Joye it took his juniors about seven weeks to read *Dracula*. He read most of the book to them, using his powerful voice to capture their attention and interest. "The kids," he told her with pride, "think it's the best book they've ever read."

Joye didn't disagree. Some of the juniors had told her that. Her concern was with how many of them would continue to read when they didn't have Fran's worksheets or Gary's voice to help them. She was concerned also with students such as those whose cumulative files she carried with her on her way to Bill Kenniston's desk: five more students with low reading scores who were failing classes in the English Department. Like most of the student body at Memorial, these students were from working-class homes with few books and little encouragement for reading. Joye's conviction was that the English program at Memorial was sadly out of tune with the needs, interests, and abilities of the students.

Today she would try one more time to get Bill to understand the problem. She already knew how he would react. He would stroke his gray beard and talk about needing a reading teacher on the staff. Joye knew that the program required rethinking, not a staff member with whom the lowest achieving students would undoubtedly be placed. She just didn't know how to get the faculty to see it her way.

CASE 4.10: CENSORSHIP
IN THE ONEIDA SCHOOL DISTRICT

Ken McKean didn't regret having been promoted from principal of Mountain Road Elementary School to assistant superintendent of the Oneida School District. The job, however, was much tougher than he had expected it to be. He had spent most of his career in education in the Oneida District. He knew everyone, including Superintendent of Schools Ron Luber, a "good old boy" if there ever was one.

Each year for the past five years the rumors about Luber's impending retirement had circulated at the beginning of the school year, and each year Luber had announced in April or May that he "wasn't ready to be put out to pasture yet." But it had become clear to Ken, and to others in the district, that Luber no longer had the zest for administration he once had. Luber was inclined to sacrifice principles for the sake of avoiding controversy, especially with community groups. Though Ken owed Ron a great deal, including his promotion to assistant superintendent, he was inclined to agree with those who hoped this year would, finally, be Luber's last.

Ken didn't know how much support he could expect from Luber with these censorship problems. Last winter, when a few parents had complained about some supplemental readings in the seventh-grade social studies curriculum, Luber had requested that the readings be omitted. Ken was uneasy about the alacrity with which Luber had given in. Success at the junior high school seemed to encourage more complaints. The Reverend Barnes of the Oneida Christian Church had given a sermon about books in schools that contradict the values of the family and the church. Letters from about twenty parents to the superintendent followed. Many of the letters referred to the eighth-grade health class. It was no wonder that teachers at the junior high school became a little paranoid, so much so that by the last month of school, two of them had called Ken to ask whether they could show specific films that had typically been part of the curriculum.

Fortunately, summer break arrived before the issue really heated up.

Ken took advantage of the summer lull and spent some time reading. He got put his old textbook from school law and read about freedom of speech and censorship. He read articles in professional journals. He began to understand what people might mean when they referred to "secular humanism." He read "The Humanist Manifesto." He found the Library Bill of Rights developed by the American Library Association. He reread the Oneida School District board policy manual regarding instructional materials and parental complaints. (See Exhibit A.)

Exhibit A: Excerpt from policy manual,
Board of Education of the Oneida Public Schools
4.45. Policies on Instructional Materials

> **4.451.** Instructional materials should be consistent with the educational goals of the school district.
>
> **4.452.** Instructional materials should be of high quality.
>
> **4.453.** Instructional materials should be selected to be appropriate for the subject area and for the age, maturity, ability, and social development of the students.
>
> **4.454.** Instructional materials should be selected so that they represent the gender, religious, ethnic, and cultural diversity of the community and the nation.
>
> **4.455.** Instructional materials that deal with controversial issues should be selected so that a balanced perspective is presented to students.
>
> **4.456.** Specific procedures shall be developed so that parents and other citizens in the school district who object to specific instructional materials will be able to bring their concerns to the attention of the school board and school district administrators and teachers.

Ken then talked to the district's four librarians and the lawyer for the school district. He ordered some videotapes on the fundamentalist movement in the United States. He read literature from People for the American Way and from the Voice of Informed Parents (VIP). And he took time to think.

Toward the end of July, Ken felt he was ready to draft a new set of procedures for handling parent complaints about curriculum materials. When he mentioned his intent to Superintendent Luber, Luber told him to go ahead but said that he, also, had some ideas about what should be done and he would present them at the first administrators' meeting in August. Ken knew he had to be ready with a plan of his own.

At the administrators' meeting, Luber began the item on parent complaints with a statement of his own position. "When these people come in with complaints about the health curriculum," he said, "I think we should tell them that we will exempt their children from the program this year and that we're looking at alternatives for the next school year."

"But what if they have their own materials they want us to use?" Ken asked.

"Then we'll include them," Luber answered.

Ken chose his words carefully. "I recommend that we follow the district policy on parent complaints about curriculum materials. I've done a great deal of reading and thinking about this issue during the summer, and I think the consequences of circumventing policy could be intense community conflict."

In the discussion that followed, everyone had something to add. Theresa Garcia, now principal of Mountain Road Elementary, said she had been amazed when a parent had objected to pictures in one of the reading books that showed a boy doing dishes, a girl raking leaves, and a girl washing a car. The parent argued that those pictures reinforce "gender neutralization." Butch Bronson, principal at the junior high school, said that he considered himself a humanist and he was convinced that the fundamentalist parents he had dealt with used the word to refer to anything they disagreed with. After 30 minutes of discussion, Ken made his final point. "I'm sure that caving in to these people will not make the problem go away." When Ken replayed the meeting in his head later, he was amazed at how easy it was to carry the argument. Luber really didn't seem to care any longer. He had been looking for an easy way out, and his judgment was that giving in was easy. Because Ken and the others seemed to feel strongly that the district should not give in, Luber simply changed his views. He had yielded to Ken. Fortunately, Ken thought, I was prepared.

Ken had outlined for the others some procedures he felt would be responsive to the concerns of parents without jeopardizing the district's responsibilities to protect freedom of speech and to resist censorship. He recommended that principals who received requests from parents to review the curriculum give the parents the curriculum guide and talk with them about it. If they asked for curriculum materials to review briefly, they should be shown the materials. If they wished to examine the materials at some length, their requests should be referred to Ken along with the form "Request for Review of Instructional Materials." (See Exhibit B.)

Parents who requested that their children be exempted from a school or class activity on the grounds that the activity conflicts with "fundamental values or religious beliefs" should have their requests honored. Students should not, however, be exempted from activities that they don't like or simply do not wish to do. Parents who asked to substitute their own materials for those used by teachers should be informed that the school cannot substitute unapproved materials. Those parents should be referred to Ken if they wished to pursue the issue.

Exhibit B: Request for Review of Instructional Materials
Oneida Public Schools

Author _____

Title _____

Publisher/Producer _____

Request initiated by _____

Address _____

_____ Zip code _____

Telephone _____

Are you the parent or guardian of students in the Oneida Public Schools?

_____

    1. What do you object to in the materials? Please be specific.

        _____

        _____

    2. What do you feel might be the result of reading or viewing the material?

        _____

        _____

    3. Did you read or view the entire work? If not, why not?

        _____

        _____

    4. What action would you recommend be taken with regard to these materials?

        _____

        _____

        Signature _____ Date _____

Ken also reminded the principals that many problems could be avoided if they and their teachers were very careful about materials that they used with classes. Everything should be previewed and should relate to specific objectives in the curriculum guides. Principals and teachers should make every effort to inform parents about the curriculum and should work *with* parents, not against them. Efforts to keep parents uninformed are more likely to create suspicion than prevent trouble, Ken had argued.

Finally, Ken argued that it was very likely that the criticisms directed at the district would continue unless the critics were provided with some sort of forum for their ideas. Ken recommended that a citizens' group be appointed to examine the current board policy on curriculum materials and then to discuss issues related to censorship and freedom of speech. The group should represent the variety of convictions in the community and should include teachers, administrators, parents, and interested patrons of the school district, including businesspeople from the community. In two or three open hearings, the advisory group could provide a forum for concerned parents and patrons without getting the school board or administrators into a public debate with single-issue groups. Ken recommended that rules be developed for these open meetings so that the comments of any one person would be limited to less than ten minutes.

The other administrators at the cabinet meeting had agreed with Ken's recommendations and suggested that Superintendent Luber take them to the school board at the August meeting. In fact, the administrators had not just agreed with Ken, they had vigorously supported him. Butch had ended the meeting on a revivalist note. "We can't avoid these controversies," he said. "Every school district in the country is experiencing them, even those that have tried to give in. We've got to stand tall, meet the issue head on, and work through it as a community. The board will soon learn that those parents who see the school as an enemy do not represent the majority of our constituents."

Ken found himself wanting to applaud.

CASE 4.11: SEX EDUCATION
IN THE RAYMONDVILLE SCHOOL DISTRICT

Lynette Darnell, science supervisor for the Raymondville District, was in her office preparing for the next day's workshop for teachers assigned to the new Human Growth and Development curriculum. School had been underway for less than two months, but if the new curriculum were to be in place by the spring, it was necessary to continue working with junior high school science and home economics teachers and a small group of substitute teachers who were also assigned to the program. The first inservice session had been held two weeks before and marked the initiation of a new program in sex education, an issue that had been troubling the Raymondville Schools for at least three years.

"Human Growth and Development." By now almost everyone recognized that these words were used to mean sex education, but in a form palatable to the Raymondville community. The district's philosophy regarding the Human Growth and Development curriculum was that it should help students "acquire knowledge and responsible decision-making skills related to physical, social, and emotional aspects of personal maturation, human sexuality, and family life."

Lynn had been involved in developing the curriculum from the beginning. She had been an observer during the meetings of the Citizens' Task Force on Human Growth and Development, a group of 30 teachers, administrators, parents, and other community members appointed to examine the district's current curriculum and to define areas in which it should be revised. She had sat through endless public hearings, and she had been party to the behind-the-scenes compromises that finally allowed the Task Force to present the superintendent with a majority report that included several specific recommendations for change. It had not been easy, but the high rate of teenage pregnancy in Raymondville and several abductions and instances of sexual abuse had led to agreement among many Task Force members that the school district had to do more to help children cope with their developing sexuality.

When the school board approved a resolution to establish a new curriculum for the seventh and eighth grades, Lynn was one of three staff members assigned to work with the board's Instruction Committee. She and her colleagues drafted objectives for the curriculum from the vague and sometimes contradictory agreements that the Instruction Committee developed, and she gathered instructional materials for examination by a board-appointed advisory committee on the Human Growth and Development curriculum. According to school board policy, all instructional materials selected for use in the Human Growth and Development curriculum had to be approved by the Instruction Committee. In practice, that meant that materials had to be previewed and approved by both the Advisory Committee and the Instruction Committee, a tedious and sometimes almost impossible process. It was difficult to find materials that satisfied both the advocates of family planning and the most convinced right-to-life members without offending those Task Force members who were determined that the new curriculum would have substance.

During the summer, Lynn's primary assignments had been to write the teaching units for nine-week courses at the seventh- and eighth-grade levels and to develop training modules for the teachers who would present the curriculum to students beginning in the spring. It hadn't been easy. The focus was to be on decision making while avoiding the specter of "values clarification," a term that had surfaced more than once in discussion of the preliminary outlines Lynn had presented to the Instruction Committee. The curriculum was developed to incorporate nontraditional teaching methods, but Lynn knew that most of the teachers who would be presenting it would be uncomfortable, especially at first, with some of the recommended approaches.

She reviewed the agenda for the next day's workshop. Assistant Superintendent David Innaway would discuss the school district's policy on the study of controversial issues (see Exhibit A). David was a consummate bureaucrat, but Lynn knew that he would present the material well and that he would encourage questions from the group.

Exhibit A: Policies of the Raymondville Public School District
6.22. The Study of Controversial Issues

6.221. Controversial issues arise from conflicts within the cherished interests, beliefs, or affiliations of large groups of our citizens. Such issues involve important proposals or policies upon which our citizens hold different points of view. The American heritage and our established traditions are not controversial. Most of the school curriculum is composed of established truths and accepted values.

Free discussion of controversial issues is the heart of the democratic process. Freedom of speech and free access to information are among our most cherished traditions. Only through the study of such issues—political, economic, or social—does youth develop abilities needed for citizenship in our democracy.

6.222. Without minimizing the importance of established truths and values, it shall be the policy of the Raymondville Public Schools to foster dispassionate, unprejudiced, scientific studies of controversial issues in an atmosphere free from bias and prejudice.

6.223. The teacher shall serve as an impartial moderator and shall not attempt either directly or indirectly to limit or control the judgment of students on controversial issues. It is the intent of this policy that the teacher shall foster the study of such issues rather than teach a particular viewpoint in regard to them.

6.224. The above policy defines the study of controversial issues in terms of the rights of students rather than in terms of the rights of teachers. Students shall have the right to study issues which are in accordance with their maturity, shall have the right of free access to all relevant materials, including those which circulate freely in the community, shall have the right to study under competent instruction in an atmosphere free from partisanship, and shall have the right to express their own opinions on controversial issues without jeopardizing relationships with their teachers or the school.

In the second part of the workshop, Lynn's co-author and fellow supervisor Donna Morgan would introduce the "Ground Rules for Human Growth and Development" that she and Lynn had developed (see Exhibit

B) and the list of prohibited practices that the Instruction Committee had insisted upon (see Exhibit C). Donna was a dynamic speaker. She would include interesting examples and help people feel comfortable with the issues.

Exhibit B: Ground Rules for the Human Growth and
Development Curriculum in Raymondville Public Schools
In order to achieve the goals of Human Growth and Development, teachers must be certain that students feel at ease in the classroom. By establishing ground rules, teachers can better ensure a comfortable atmosphere in which discussion can take place.

1. Everyone is free to ask questions.
2. Everyone has the right to "pass" on activities or on answering questions any time they feel uncomfortable. However, total class participation is encouraged.
3. Students are to be sensitive toward classmates with different points of view. It is all right for students to disagree, but not to "put each other down."
4. Confidentiality is a must. Students are not to quote others outside of the class.
5. There is to be no talking about class members outside of class.
6. Students are to speak for themselves. They are to use "I" messages to state feelings or opinions.
7. No question is a dumb question. Questions only indicate the desire for knowledge; they do not tell anything else about the person asking the question.
8. Whenever possible, correct terminology should be used.
9. Students are encouraged to discuss the issues raised in class with their parents and to give parents an accurate account of what the class is about.

Exhibit C:
The Human Growth and Development Program will NOT

1. Deal with or provide information on abortion.
2. Discuss homosexuality or other deviant lifestyles.
3. Promote being sexually active nor tell students it is "okay" to engage in sexual activities.
4. Penalize children whose parents "opt" them out of the program.
5. Utilize information or materials that parents have not had an opportunity to preview.
6. Replace the churches' responsibility or obligation to teach and interpret what is right and what is wrong.

Just before a lunch break, Lynn would lead the group in a demonstration of one of the opening activities for the seventh-grade course, strategies in decision making. She would present the following guide to decision making:

1. Define the problem to be solved in a few sentences. Define it in personal terms such as "How do I . . . ?" and "What will I . . . ?"
2. Educate yourself. Gather information related to the problem. Then identify at least three possible solutions or alternatives.
3. List the positive and negative aspects of each alternative. What is the best thing that can happen? What is the worst thing that can happen?
4. List persons affected by these alternatives and any personal values that may be in conflict with these alternatives.
5. Compare all the alternatives and identify your choice.
6. Design a plan to carry out this decision.

Then the teachers would be asked to gather in small groups and discuss one of several dilemmas that had been written for the seventh grade. The discussion should follow the decision-making guide and give teachers experience with the activity they would be using with their students.

After a break for lunch, the workshop would continue with a session on understanding adolescence, presented by one of the school nurses and a school district psychologist. The workshop would conclude with a demonstration of two more activities that would be included in the curriculum materials.

It would be a full day. But Lynn was amazed at the willingness of the school district to hire substitute teachers, release the regular teachers from a full day of teaching to receive training in the curriculum, and even provide lunch. One thing she had learned about curriculum related to controversial issues was this: given a hot topic, the district could find money to support the kind of training Lynn felt should be standard practice when new curricula were developed.

Case 4.11: Part II

The morning half of the workshop had gone pretty well. David had been reasonably entertaining and absolutely clear. Donna's presentation had been expertly done, though teachers had not discussed the issues much or raised many questions. They had, however, participated enthusiastically in the demonstration that Lynn led. Now, after lunch and time to wander around the courtyard at Southeast High School, the group reconvened with questions about the morning presentations.

Joan Radcliffe, a science teacher at Midvale Junior High School, asked the first question. "Isn't this just sex education with a new name?"

"No," Lynn responded. "I don't think so. The focus of this program is on responsible behavior, respect for self and others, the enhancement of self-esteem, and the development and use of decision-making skills. None of those values was the focus of the old sex education curriculum."

Wilma Solomon raised her hand. "I've been looking over the materials we've received so far, and I can't find any reference to a textbook for students."

"Remember from our first meeting," Lynn began patiently, "that teachers will be provided with all the materials in a loose-leaf binder. There will be no textbook for students. Handouts that can be duplicated will be provided for all approved activities."

"What if I need more information about a topic?" Wilma continued.

"We'll include a list of suggested references for each topic and make sure those references are available through the Professional Library."

"My concern," began Jeremy Phillips, science teacher at Kirkwell Middle School, "is that I won't feel comfortable or know how to react when students talk about their own experiences with parents and families very different from my parents and my family. I could teach sex education. I'm not sure I can lead discussions in which students may tell some really gruesome stories."

Donna responded. "We want to emphasize from the first days of the Human Growth and Development course that students are responsible for self-disclosure. We will have to help them to distinguish between appropriate and inappropriate self-disclosure. We will need to discourage them from disclosing the private experiences of family members and friends."

"Easy to say," Jeremy said, "but I can guarantee you that the inappropriate will be disclosed. I can even tell you which seventh graders are most likely to say something inappropriate, especially if they think they can shock the rest of the class."

"We'll need to feel our way with this," Donna replied. "Keep emphasizing the ground rules. Go over them carefully each day during the first week."

"I'm feeling my own dilemma," began Ramonna Dawson, home economics teacher from Burton Junior High School. "The ground rules say that 'no question is a dumb question' and that 'everyone is free to ask questions,' but the list of prohibited practices tells me that we can't talk about homosexuality and that we can't talk about abortion. I can guarantee that those topics will come up, especially if we can establish the free and open atmosphere in the classroom that you're telling us we need to have."

Lynn responded. "If this occurs, then simply say to the student, 'The policy of the school district does not permit us to discuss that issue.'"

"Are you kidding? That will turn kids off immediately," Ramonna replied. "I ask them to be open and feel free to ask their 'dumbest' questions but then turn around and tell them we can't talk about it."

"But you can't talk about it," Lynn reminded the group. "The school board has given us very little latitude here. Maybe the next time we teach the course, after we have shown that it can be done. Maybe next year, when this isn't such a touchy issue in the community. But for now, we have to follow the policy."

"Never mind that the policy doesn't make sense."

The comment came from the back of the room, and Lynn wasn't sure who said it. She didn't know how to respond, so she pretended she hadn't heard and began to introduce the speakers on understanding adolescence.

CHAPTER 5

Managing Resources

There is a New Golden Rule becoming popular which goes something like: He who has the gold makes the rules.

Jeffery Peffer

CASE 5.1: SYMBOLIC DECISION IN INVERNESS

Board president Ames Barkley sat impassively as Dr. William Ketner, superintendent of schools for the Inverness District, presented the major points in a school reform bill just enacted by the state legislature. Ames felt compelled to speak, however, when the last three requirements were reviewed: the district curriculum objectives had to be filed with the State Department of Education, the district had to comply with state guidelines for a comprehensive testing program, and school report cards giving information about the collective achievement of students had to be issued to parents for each school in the district.

Ames asked his question with indignation in his voice. "Dr. Ketner, how much do you expect those last three items to cost the district?"

"We've computed the cost for those three items at approximately $25,000."

"That's not a lot of money compared with our total budget, but I object to continued mandates from our legislature without funding to implement them. Therefore, I would entertain a motion that we express our displeasure with the continuation of this behavior."

Brenda Goddard, treasurer of the board, indicated she wished to speak. "President Barkley, I concur wholeheartedly with you. I move to ignore the state requirements concerning curriculum objectives, student testing, and school report cards."

Rollin Sidwell seconded Brenda's motion.

In the lively discussion that followed, board members agreed that the issue was more symbolic than fiscal. Inverness already had curriculum objectives, and no one could see any reason why they should be filed with the State Department of Education. The testing program in the school district was more than adequate, and information about student performance had been shared with the public even before the state had encouraged district testing programs. Brenda's motion passed unanimously.

Ames couldn't resist a bit of commentary. "I'm pleased to see that the board is of one mind on this issue. That doesn't happen too often. But I, for one, don't know how we can support unfunded state mandates when we're being forced to make drastic budget cuts, including laying off 75 employees to curtail our budget deficit."

When Ames talked to the education reporter for the local newspaper after the meeting, he was more expansive. "We agreed that this was something we wanted to do philosophically and symbolically as much as financially. How fair is it for the state to require us to comply with new regulations while reducing the amount of fiscal support? This business of doing more with less has to stop sometime."

News reports on the Inverness Board's action were carried widely in the state papers, and a small story appeared in a national education newsletter. Reactions from other local school administrators were mixed, with some praising the symbolic gesture and some criticizing it.

CASE 5.2: THE CANDY SALE

Carol Gilligan had known when she accepted the position as the first principal of Shoreline Elementary School that the job wouldn't be easy. At the same time, she couldn't have imagined some of the problems she faced during that first year—things people had never talked about in the leadership classes she had taken at the university.

For example, she never could have anticipated the problems with the candy sale. She knew that the district had very limited funds and that the building would open without really being finished. She had insisted that the district pave the playground area, but there was no money for playground equipment. Ed Hartnip, director of buildings and grounds for the school district, had told her that the equipment would have to wait until the next year. What she hadn't anticipated was how determined the board members of the Parent-Teacher Organization would be to equip the playground immediately.

The PTO board met during the first month of school and, without her support, passed a motion to purchase equipment and hold a fund-raiser to cover the cost. Carol, who had attended the board meeting, had indicated that she did not want to get into the fund-raising business during the first few months of school. The board president, Wilma Boyd, interpreted that to mean that Carol didn't feel she had the time, and Wilma offered to make contacts with other schools and identify a fund-raising activity that could be done quickly and would provide the money needed. Carol had reluctantly agreed that Wilma could investigate fund-raising possibilities and report back to the board in two weeks.

When the board met two weeks later, Wilma began the meeting by introducing Russell Solokow, the local agent for a national fund-raising company, who had worked with other schools in the district. Wilma also announced that she and her husband, Mike, and the Stephens, also Shoreline parents, were willing to loan the PTO $5,000 for the purchase of playground equipment on the understanding that the money would be repaid after the fund-raiser. The other board members applauded, and Solokow launched into his spiel. He recommended a candy sale. He said that a school the size of Shoreline could easily raise over $5,000 in a two-week period, and he described the products his company offered and the prizes that children could earn.

When the group asked Carol what she thought, she replied that she had reservations about the candy sale. First, she was bothered by the idea of using kids to raise funds for the school. Second, she was concerned about the safety of children who would have to go out into the community to sell candy.

Solokow replied that he and his company discouraged the use of door-to-door sales. He recommended that the board adopt a rule against door-to-door sales and said that he would emphasize that rule in his presentation to the children. Children, he said, could easily sell the candy to friends, neighbors, and relatives without contacting strangers.

Several board members responded to Carol's concerns about using the children in a fund-raiser. Martha Simmons argued that the experience would be a great learning experience, that the children would learn to handle money and work toward a goal. Two of the teachers attending the meeting agreed. Nancy Steiner said that a project such as this would get the children to work together. In fact, she said, the candy sale was just the sort of project that would bring people in the school together, including the many children from military families who were new to the community. At the end of the discussion, the board voted unanimously to accept the loan of $5,000, order the playground equipment, and begin preparations for a candy sale in mid-October. Wilma closed the meeting by telling Carol not to worry, that the PTO board would handle all the arrangements.

On the morning of the assembly to kick off the candy sale, Carol met with Russell Solokow before the children gathered in the gymnasium. She reminded him that she and the PTO board were concerned about door-to-door sales and that he needed to emphasize the rule in his presentation to the children. Solokow agreed. Carol watched from the back of the room while Solokow explained the rules for the candy sale and then held up the tape recorder, the camera, and the cassette tapes that the children could win by selling a certain number of boxes of candy. She had wondered at the time which message was stronger, the one about the rules or the one that encouraged children to work for the prizes. Solokow concluded by reminding them that they had only two weeks and that they could pick up boxes of candy at the end of the school day.

Carol had to admit that the parents organized the sale well. Volunteers showed up every day to collect money from the children at the beginning of the school day and to distribute boxes of candy at the end of the day. Posters reporting sales for each classroom and the names of children who had sold enough boxes to qualify for prizes were posted in the lobby. As if on cue, the playground equipment was delivered and installed two days after sales began.

Problems really didn't start until the beginning of the second week. On Monday Carol received calls from two parents saying that their children had been threatened by other children because they weren't selling enough candy. One father who called said that his son had been told by an older child that he wouldn't be able to use the playground equipment because he had sold only three boxes. If that weren't enough, competition for the individual prizes had become intense. On Tuesday Carol was told that children were selling candy door-to-door, especially children from the military base. Carol wasn't surprised when she thought about it. What friends, neighbors, or relatives would provide a ready market for children who had only recently moved to town?

Carol passed the candy distribution table on her way through the lobby after school on Tuesday. Wilma was handing out boxes and encouraging children to keep up their good work. She stopped Carol and said that she had a lot of ideas about how to organize next year's candy sale. Carol replied, "There won't be a candy sale next year," and continued on to her meeting with the third-grade teachers.

CASE 5.3: BUDGET CUTS
IN THE SOUTHBOROUGH SCHOOLS

The last item on the principals' bimonthly meeting with the superintendent was anticipated shortfalls in state funds. Superintendent of Schools Maureen Howard reported that Southborough District had received notice from the state commissioner of education about the effects on education of anticipated declines in state revenue. All indications were that the legislature would appropriate slightly less for education than had been appropriated in the previous budget year. The commissioner asked that superintendents and boards think about the impact on budgets for the coming fiscal year and begin planning in case fewer resources were available.

Superintendent Howard said that the best estimate that she and her staff could come up with from the numbers being tossed around in the legislature was that each building in the district could anticipate a 3 percent loss in operating budget. She acknowledged that principals had just submitted their budget plans for the next year, but she asked that each reconsider the budget in light of these anticipated cuts and prepare two items before the next principals' meeting: (1) criteria by which the operating budget could be cut, and (2) specific suggested reductions.

Steve Gamble, principal at Southborough High School, and Jill Varner, new principal at Central Park Elementary, walked out of the meeting together. "Well, neighbor," Steve began, "welcome to the real world of rational planning. We just turned our budgets in, and already we have to rework them."

"I'm confused, Steve. What exactly is it that Superintendent Howard wants? It sounds as if I'm going to have to start all over."

"It's not as bad as that, Jill. Look, I'd be glad to drop by Central Park sometime in the next few days, and we can have a strategy session."

"I'd appreciate it, Steve. Let me know when you have a few minutes."

Three days later, Steve walked from the high school to Central Park to discuss the budgets. Jill laid her proposed budget on the table. (See Exhibit A.)

Steve took his budget from the folder he had brought with him and handed it to Jill. (See Exhibit B.)

"Jill," Steve began, "we haven't had to do this for a long time. I thought we were beyond this kind of instant reaction to messages from the commissioner."

"We are reacting to conjecture, aren't we," Jill replied. "We don't really know that cuts will be necessary. The legislature may come through. Shouldn't we make an effort to change their minds rather than assuming that the cuts will be made?"

"I'm sure that the state education lobbyists are working on it. In the meantime, we need to think through what we'll tell the superintendent. My concern is that if we show that we can live with a 3 percent reduction, the board may conclude that our proposed budgets are too high."

"Our budgets are certainly different, Steve. What criteria do you suggest we use that will work for both of us?"

"One way I've dealt with this before is to propose to cut items that booster clubs may pay for if the district can't."

"That doesn't help me much. The only booster club I have is the parents' organization, and their position is that they won't raise money to support the operating budget for the school. You know, I'm just now

EXHIBIT A
CENTRAL PARK ELEMENTARY SCHOOL PROPOSED BUDGET, NEXT FISCAL YEAR

Object Code	Item of Expenditure	Proposed Amount
110–000–334	Field trips	$ 1,250
110–000–410	Supplies	16,104
110–000–420	Textbooks	8,915
110–000–530	Furniture and equipment	2,000
110–000–664	Computer supplies	2,000
110–000–665	Computer equipment	3,750
110–000–693	Inservice	2,800
110–050–410	Science supplies	300
110–059–410	Outdoor education supplies	2,000
110–068–410	Physical education supplies	525
110–070–695	Office equipment	1,450
110–090–410	Art supplies	250
110–093–410	Vocal music supplies	250
110–094–410	Instrumental music supplies	250
110–094–695	Instrumental music repair	150
	Total	**$41,994**

EXHIBIT B
SOUTHBOROUGH SENIOR HIGH SCHOOL PROPOSED BUDGET, NEXT FISCAL YEAR

Object Code	Item of Expenditure	Proposed Amount
110–000–410	Supplies	$ 34,000
110–000–420	Textbooks	1,000
110–000–530	Furniture and equipment	6,000
110–000–660	Data processing	1,000
110–000–664	Computer supplies	1,621
110–000–665	Computer equipment	5,745
110–000–693	Inservice	9,500
110–000–695	Repair and replacement	200
110–010–410	English supplies	5,641
110–010–420	English textbooks	6,408
110–010–530	English furniture and equipment	1,235
110–012–410	Drama supplies	12,400
110–012–420	Drama textbooks	100
110–012–530	Drama furniture and equipment	500
110–012–695	Drama repair and replacement	500

SOUTHBOROUGH SENIOR HIGH SCHOOL PROPOSED
BUDGET *(CONTINUED)*

Object Code	Item of Expenditure	Proposed Amount
110-013-410	Debate supplies	4,000
110-013-420	Debate textbooks	800
110-014-410	Journalism supplies	8,341
110-014-530	Journalism furniture	652
110-014-695	Journalism repair and replacement	270
110-015-410	Reading supplies	599
110-019-410	Learning center	3,500
110-029-410	Foreign language supplies	4,480
110-029-420	Foreign language textbooks	216
110-030-410	Social studies supplies	2,643
110-030-420	Social studies textbooks	4,694
110-030-530	Social studies furniture, equipment	1,794
110-040-410	Math supplies	2,083
110-040-420	Math textbooks	4,000
110-040-530	Math furniture and equipment	1,575
110-050-410	Science supplies	9,805
110-050-420	Science textbooks	95
110-050-530	Science furniture and equipment	4,239
110-050-695	Science repair and replacement	400
110-060-410	Home economics supplies	4,367
110-060-420	Home economics textbooks	1,172
110-060-530	Home economics furniture, equipment	980
110-060-695	Home economics repair and replacement	150
110-068-410	Physical education supplies	2,148
110-068-420	Physical education textbooks	345
110-068-695	Physical education repair and replacement	800
110-079-410	Career education supplies	2,000
110-080-410	Industrial arts supplies	5,936
110-080-420	Industrial arts textbooks	139
110-080-530	Industrial arts furniture and equipment	8,894
110-080-695	Industrial arts repair and replacement	2,581
110-082-410	Vocational business supplies	5,833
110-082-420	Vocational business textbooks	240
110-082-695	Vocational business repair and replacement	1,000
110-083-410	Vocational business grant supplies	26,024
110-090-410	Art supplies	9,675
110-093-410	Vocal music supplies	7,865
110-093-530	Vocal music furniture, equipment	3,600
110-093-695	Vocal music repair, replacement	1,355
110-094-410	Instrumental music supplies	6,400
110-094-420	Instrumental music textbooks	1,300
110-094-530	Instrumental music furniture, equipment	2,700
110-094-695	Instrumental music repair, replacement	2,000
110-097-410	Fine arts supplies	314
110-098-410	Pep club supplies	1,000
	Total	**$238,854**

thinking about how I'm going to defend these cuts to upset parents and teachers. Let's get serious."

"Jill, I was serious. But if you want a more general principle, you could think about how many students would be affected."

"So that means I cut vocal and instrumental music supplies and you cut debate."

"Well, not necessarily, though we do have a debate booster club that's pretty supportive of the program. Debate is a good possibility. I really do take alternative sources of funds into account."

"What about cutting those expenditures that can be delayed a year?"

"Good idea, Jill. You might also think about avoiding cuts that would have the most long-term impact."

"Okay. Now the problem is to figure out how those principles apply to these budgets."

"Give it some thought. Maybe we can meet again about this before we have to report back to the superintendent. Right now, though, I need to get back to the high school for a meeting. Thanks for the coffee."

CASE 5.4: BALANCING PER PUPIL EXPENDITURES

Constance Mabrey, superintendent of Haven Crest School District, picked up the morning paper. The headlines in the state section drew her attention to an article about the Edgemont School District, a district in a neighboring county with which Constance was very familiar.

Nixon Crocker, the superintendent in Edgemont, was a friend and colleague. They had become better acquainted in recent months as the two school districts faced similar problems. Both districts had limited financial resources. Both had adopted plans that required transporting students for racial balance. Both had been under court orders to desegregate schools since the mid-1970s. Edgemont had recently petitioned for removal of the court order.

The judge who examined Edgemont's petition had responded by identifying two necessary actions before she would lift the court order. First, the assignments of teachers had to be balanced by race and experience. Second, lower per pupil spending in predominantly black schools had to be remedied.

As Nixon had explained to Constance, the disparities in Edgemont had resulted from rapid growth in predominantly black schools. To meet the increased enrollments, younger and less experienced—and thus lower-paid—teachers had been hired. These teachers were mostly white. Constance and Nixon had frequently discussed their personal efforts to recruit minority teachers and the discouraging results they had been able to achieve so far. Each year fewer and fewer minority graduates were available. Constance had discussed the problem with state university administrators, but they told their own stories about intensified efforts to recruit qualified minority students into colleges of education and their own limited successes.

Constance knew that Haven Crest had its own spending disparities. The reason was different. The imbalances in Haven Crest were due in part to the location of predominantly minority schools in the oldest parts of the city, and teachers at those schools tended to be long-standing employees. In fact, per pupil expenditures had historically been higher in the central city schools. In the past few years, however, teachers at those schools had been retiring at a faster rate than teachers in the suburban schools. The result was the same as the problem the judge identified in Edgemont: more inexperienced, less expensive, and largely white teachers in the older schools, and lower per pupil expenditures.

As Nixon had worked with his administrative staff to respond to the judge's stipulations, he often talked with Constance and solicited her advice. Just before the opening of school two months earlier, Nixon had announced a plan to transfer 53 experienced teachers to the predominantly black schools. The transfers resulted in lower pupil–teacher ratios and increases in the per pupil costs at the predominantly black schools. All indications had been that the plan would satisfy the judge's concerns, though no formal ruling had been received. The teachers' association had originally announced it would oppose the transfers, but then association officers decided not to file a grievance. The newspaper story that Constance was reading added a new development. The local chapter of the National Association for the Advancement of Colored People had strongly criticized the teacher reassignments, saying that the district should have examined the specific needs of each school and developed new programs to compensate for the spending disparities.

Though nothing had become public yet, Constance and her staff were about to propose that the board adopt a plan similar to that used in Edgemont. They had been waiting to see if the judge would accept the plan as a satisfactory solution to the disparities she had identified. Constance had never been sure that the teachers' association in Haven Crest would accept the plan as easily as had been the case in Edgemont, and she had never included the association in any discussions of the proposal. Now she wasn't sure what to do. Should she proceed with the plan, hoping that local minority advocates would adopt a different position in Haven Crest? What could she do to solicit the support of the teachers' association? More important, was Nixon's plan the only option for a district that lacked the ability to balance spending without shifting resources? She just wasn't sure.

CASE 5.5: THE CONSOLIDATION ISSUE
IN THE LONE TREE DISTRICT

Claude Raines read through the paper he had just written. He felt strange being a student again, writing papers for classes instead of for board members and taxpayers, after all his years as superintendent of schools in the Lone Tree and Washington school districts. Writing this paper had been worthwhile. It had given him a chance to reflect now on the consolidation decision in Lone Tree several years after the heated emotions and conflicts in the community

Members of the Board of Education for the Lone Tree Public School District had known for several years that they would eventually be forced to dissolve the school district. The number of secondary school students (grades nine through twelve) had not exceeded 21 for several years. Because state law prohibited a school district from operating a secondary program with fewer than 25 students, the district had discontinued the program and had begun contract arrangements with three neighboring school districts for the education of those students.

Several community members were strongly opposed to consolidation. Costs in the district were comparatively low, averaging about $1,600 per pupil, compared with a state average of approximately $3,000. The tax levy was $.42 per hundred dollars of assessed valuation, compared with a state average of $1.30 per hundred. The board, however, felt that there were no options. The district could not, under law, operate a secondary school program. And without the secondary program, the district could not exist, because the law no longer permitted the establishment of elementary school districts. Moreover, only 62 elementary-age students were enrolled in the district at the time that the board decided to proceed with negotiations for consolidation with a neighboring district. Although it would be possible to contract with neighboring districts for the education of those children and convert the district to nonoperating status, the district could exist as a nonoperating district for only three years without a special petition to the State Board of Education. Board members had agreed that planning to consolidate was preferable to postponing the inevitable through conversion to a nonoperating status.

Two years of discussion had produced no clear consensus from the community about which neighboring school district should be approached about consolidation. Under the leadership of Board President Leroy Johnson, it was decided that formal negotiations should begin with the two adjacent districts, Knobby Creek and Crestridge.

The Board of Education employed an educational consultant and attorney and appointed a citizens' planning group to investigate a merger with either Knobby Creek or Crestridge. Each of these districts was asked to respond to a planning proposal developed by the planning group and the consultant. Key elements of the planning proposal were as follows:

1. Programs and staff in the Lone Tree District would continue unchanged during any school year in which consolidation took place.
2. The board of education of the consolidated district would consist of six members, two of whom would be from Lone Tree and four of whom would represent the receiving district.
3. Current assets and liabilities of the Lone Tree District would be assumed by the receiving district.
4. Bonded indebtedness that had occurred prior to merger would remain the responsibility of the original district.
5. The new district would develop a transportation plan to provide rural route service on county roads under normal operating conditions. Similar arrangements would be provided for those students living within the town of Lone Tree. Arrangements would include transportation for school activities that would not be covered by regular route service.
6. An attendance center for elementary students in kindergarten through sixth grades would be maintained within the town of Lone Tree. That center would continue until a majority of the voters decided to discontinue it or the school district decided to discontinue it if fewer than 25 students were involved.
7. To accommodate the attendance center, Lone Tree would use its cash reserves to renovate the 1960 and 1974 buildings owned by the district. The 1916 building and the gymnasium would be turned over to a community nonprofit organization. The school district would retain priority use rights to the gymnasium.
8. The receiving district would ensure that several program considerations would be met:
   a. A leadership management team would be formed to provide for administration, fiscal and budget management, and supervision of operations and maintenance. That team would include the current superintendent of Lone Tree.
   b. The district elementary teaching staff would be organized in kindergarten through six grade to provide an optimal class size of 20–25 students per grade level or 15–20 students for combined grades.
   c. The district secondary teaching staff would be organized in grades seven through twelve to provide an optimal class size of 20–25 students.
   d. The consolidated district would provide comprehensive educational programs in mathematics, science, language arts, social studies, and foreign language.
   e. Support staff would be available in guidance, media, speech therapy, health services, and special education.

   f. The district would have programs in business education, home economics, computer technology, and general shop.

   g. The district would have a fine arts program, including vocal and instrumental music and art.

   h. Athletic programs would include major team and individual sports such as football, basketball, volleyball, track and field.

   i. Services would be provided to all students at all attendance areas as building and facilities permitted.

9. Families located on the edges of the attendance area for the consolidated district could request contracting privileges with a closer district, provided that doing so was in the best interests of the students.

10. Secondary school students currently attending districts other than the consolidating district would have the option of completing their programs through tuition arrangements.

11. Information about the anticipated district budget of expenditures, per pupil costs, and tax levy would be provided.

When the citizens' committee received responses to the planning document from Knobby Creek and Crestridge, two of the members compiled the information into a table of comparisons.

After examining the table and discussing the responses from Knobby Creek and Crestridge, members of the citizens' committee generally

COMPARISON OF KNOBBY CREEK AND CRESTRIDGE RESPONSES

Item	Knobby Creek	Crestridge
1. Continuing programs at mid-year	yes	yes
2. Composition of board	4–2 okay	5–1 proposed
3. Bonded indebtedness	agree	agree
4. Transportation	agree	agree
5. K–6 attendance center in Lone Tree	agree	agree
6. Program considerations	agree to all	agree to all except provision of all services at all sites
7. Families at edge of district	agree	agree
8. Tuition for current secondary students attending another district	agree	agree
9. Current district enrollment	141, K–12	512, K–12
10. Current per pupil expenditures	$4,669	$3,130
11. Current tax levy	$1.35 per hundred dollars valuation	$.923 per hundred dollars valuation
12. Anticipated per pupil expenditures	$3,300	$2,600
13. Anticipated general tax levy dollar	$.92–.97 per hundred dollars valuation	$.75–.77 per hundred dollars valuation

agreed that the best choice would be merger with Crestridge. That was the recommendation they took to the Board of Education.

The primary source of information for residents of the Town of Lone Tree, outside of informal conversations in the local cafe, was the *Lone Tree Messenger*, a weekly newspaper owned and operated by Gil and Marietta Bromley, former residents of Knobby Creek. Editorials in the paper opposed consolidation with Crestridge, arguing that the school district was too big, nearly four times as large as Knobby Creek. Lone Tree students were accustomed to individual attention, the editorials argued, and they would not get it in the Crestridge District. The editorials also noted the unwillingness of the Crestridge board to appoint two Lone Tree members. It was unlikely that Lone Tree residents would be able to influence what happened in the consolidated district. While the editorial coverage was extensive, very little of the information from the planning proposals was reported in news stories. Two influential town residents, a local veterinarian and the owner of the lumber yard, both were strong proponents of merger with Crestridge. Each wrote a letter to the editor of the local paper, but neither letter was published.

The citizens' committee recommendation was received by the Lone Tree Board of Education at a meeting in early February. While most board members supported the committee's recommendation and the others were neutral, the board had decided to poll the voters about their support for consolidation with Crestridge. The final tally was 157 votes in favor of consolidation and 158 votes against. At a heated board meeting in April many citizens indicated that the vote had not provided the board with a clear mandate for action. The board decided to abide by the community vote.

When that occurred, Raines had offered his resignation as superintendent. And that was the end of his part of the story. He had done all he could. He felt the board made the wrong decision. Consolidation with Crestridge would have provided the most opportunities for Lone Tree students and at the most reasonable cost. Consolidation itself was inevitable, and he was unwilling to go through the process again. He left the district for the Washington Public Schools. Until he began writing the paper, he had never looked back.

CASE 5.6: IS IT FAIR TO TREAT JULIUS AS SPECIAL?

When the third-grade teachers at Oak Valley Elementary School met to discuss Julius Fuentes, no one had any new ideas. It wasn't the first time Julius had been discussed by the staff at Oak Valley. Once again Julius's teacher, this year Lenore Provo, had recommended that he be tested for special education placement, and once again he had scored too low for placement in a resource room and not low enough to be classified as mentally handicapped, which would qualify him for placement in a special education classroom. Lenore had asked that Warner Robbins, the principal at Oak Valley, and Louise Johnson, the resource room teacher, sit in on the meeting.

Lenore described the extra help that she tried to provide for Julius. Everyone agreed that she was using appropriate strategies. "What frustrates me," said Lenore, "is that Julius can learn when I can work with him that way. The problem is that I can't do it very often. I have 28 other children to work with."

"Why don't we send Julius to the resource room to work with Louise one or two hours a week?" Christine Summerville suggested.

"He doesn't qualify for resource room," Louise replied.

"That's not a problem," Robbins replied, "as long as we don't count him among our state-reimbursed students."

"But Mr. Robbins," Louise continued, "I am working with the maximum number of students the district places in any resource room right now. In fact, the two children who qualified for services last month were transferred to another school so that they could be placed. I can't take a child who doesn't qualify when other children have had to transfer."

"I probably have five children in my classroom who could benefit from being in a resource room, but they don't qualify for services either," Dan Kenning pointed out. "Why should Julius be treated any differently...."

"Mr. Robbins," Lenore interrupted, "please think about it. Julius can learn if he gets extra help. In my classroom, he just can't get enough of it. We have to do something to help the children we can help."

CASE 5.7: "WHO DO I TALK TO NEXT?"

Mrs. Phillips was clearly angry. Elden Schreiner, principal of Surfside Elementary School, wasn't quite sure how to convince her that her daughter Jane, the youngest of the four Phillips children, would be all right. He knew that parents often were overly concerned about the last child to enter school. Mrs. Phillips, however, didn't see it his way at all.

"Mr. Schreiner," she began, "Jane brought home that letter from you last week saying that she had been placed in another first-grade class with a new teacher. That was three weeks after school started, and you didn't let us know until the day before the change was to be made. I don't understand what's happening here. Jane has been so distressed by this. She really liked Mrs. Hanson, and she's terrified of Ms. Doty."

"We had to make some adjustments, Mrs. Phillips, because we have fewer children at Surfside this fall than we thought we would have. We waited as long as we could, hoping that more children would enroll. But at last count, Mrs. Hanson had only 15 children in her classroom and our other first-grade classes all had more than 25 children in them."

"Twenty-five children is an awfully large class. Jane would have done well in a small class of 15."

"I'm sure she would, Mrs. Phillips, but a school has to be concerned about efficiency, just like any business. We have to provide quality education within our budget, and our budget won't support classes of 15 or 20."

"Now I read in the newspaper that the military may transfer several hundred families here after October 1. What will happen to all those children, Mr. Schreiner?"

"They will be assigned to classes as they arrive, just as any new children would. We couldn't wait another three weeks to adjust our classrooms. That would have been even more disconcerting for the children and the teachers."

"Jane is so shy, and she liked Mrs. Hanson so well. Why couldn't Jane just stay with her?"

"Mrs. Hanson has been transferred to Westside Elementary. I'm sure, though, that Jane will like Margaret Doty once she gets to know her. Margaret is an energetic, creative new teacher."

"Ms. Doty told me on the phone that it will take Jane two weeks to fit in. Your changes have put Janie two weeks behind the other first graders."

"I'm not sure what Margaret told you, but she probably meant that Jane will feel at home in the new class in a couple of weeks. Children adapt easily to change, Mrs. Phillips, and Jane will get to know her new classmates quickly."

"Well, I still don't understand why Janie had to move. Your concern with the budget and efficiency has caused my daughter to be scared and upset. She was so excited when school started, and now she doesn't even want to come to school. Tell me, who do I talk to next?"

CASE 5.8: CLOSING THE SHADY RIVER SCHOOL

Driving by the small, white frame building with the old bell tower, Tom Housak once again read the worn sign over the door: "School District #33, Brewster County, Est. 1890." He had been driving by Shady River Elementary School on his way to work for many years, but he had been a board member for only five years and president of the school board for two.

In the 1950s Shady River School District had stopped educating secondary school students and begun sending the older children from the district to neighboring Oak Valley. But Shady River still ran its own elementary school in this two-room building. This year the district had 19 students in kindergarten through grade six, although they had no third graders; the district employed two teachers.

The previous night's school board meeting had been the most acrimonious he had experienced in his years on the board. Twenty-five people had attended, the largest turnout anyone could remember. Interest was high because three months before, parents of students at Shady River had petitioned the board to close the school and send the students to Oak Valley. While all three board members, himself included, supported the parents' request, other members of the community had disagreed. The opponents had finally made their case at the previous night's meeting.

Mary Willis, speaking for the parents, had argued that students would have more opportunities in Oak Valley. She lauded Shady River's two teachers for their work with individual students, but she noted that Oak Valley had an instrumental music program, special activities for gifted children, and an elementary school counselor. She noted that the request to the board had been signed by every parent who would have children enrolled at Shady River the next year.

Opponents of sending the children to Oak Valley had presented a number of arguments. Margaret Stassen had said: "Shady River is a good school. My nephews did well there. A member of the county superintendent's staff told me that this school provides 'good education.'"

Another opponent of closing the school said he had learned that sending the children to Oak Valley would cost just as much as keeping the school open. Dolly Travis, the board treasurer, spoke next. She said that it was true that the district could maintain the current tax rate if the children were enrolled at Oak Valley as tuition-paying students. "If we keep Shady River open," she continued, "we will need to increase taxes in order to repair and maintain the building. Don't forget that this building is nearly a hundred years old. It needs a new roof, and that's just part of what we need to do if we're going to continue to use it."

Gladys Block said that she thought that most of those who supported the closing had only recently moved to the Shady River district, many of them from the city, and they didn't understand the importance of the school to the community. At the end of her remarks, another member of the audience called Gladys a hypocrite and pointedly noted that she had lived in the district for only a year. Several people applauded. Gladys replied that her family had owned land in the district for years and that she knew the area very well.

Marvin Johnson, a long-time supporter of the school, nearly had tears in his eyes as he spoke. "Don't you see, this problem has come between neighbors, has split families. Can't we just forget it and keep our little school?"

Jim Ramsey, parent of a fourth grader, said he and his wife had been sending their son to Oak Valley and paying the tuition themselves. "Take it from a parent who knows," he said, "it's better over there."

One of the parents proposed a compromise position: "Suspend operations at Shady River for a year and send the children to Oak Valley," she said. "Then we'll know what is best for our children."

Tom disagreed. "We've been arguing about this for months. I don't want to have to argue it again next year at this time."

Finally, Ted Crupa, board secretary, spoke. Ted rarely said anything at board meetings when anyone other than the three board members were present. "Look, I've lost a lot of sleep over this. We have a good school here, but we need to consider what's best for the children. It's kind of like having a '57 Chevy, and you've driven it for many years and you love it. But then you get to thinking about the guy over there who's got a new car with power steering."

At the end of the evening, the board finally voted 3–0 to suspend operations at the school for the upcoming year, provided Oak Valley would agree to employ Shady River's two teachers. Opponents of closing the school had the last word. One stood up at the end of the meeting and announced that he would host a meeting on Wednesday for those interested in recalling the school board president. "Tom," he said, "has been thinking about resigning for a while. It's time for us to make up his mind for him."

Tom wasn't sure yet how he felt. He wondered whether he had the energy or the will to continue the fight. His youngest son had graduated from Shady River at the end of the previous year. It was true that he had talked about resigning before the board had tackled the parents' request to close the school. At the same time, he hated to cave in when he felt he was right. Although the quality of basic education the students received in Shady River was good, they would have more choices and opportunities in Oak Valley. If the board made a bad decision, it was in deciding to suspend operations for a year rather than simply closing the school.

As he pulled his car into the parking lot outside his office, he decided that the problems at Shady River would just have to wait while he tackled the lagging sales of agricultural machinery in out-state counties.

CASE 5.9: PLACING THE NEW TEACHERS

Manuel Ortiz, personnel director for the Union City Public School District, was tired of dealing with the same problems year after year. Union City had been required by court order to achieve an appropriate minority/

majority ratio for faculty. Manuel had spent the past several years trying to bring the district into compliance. He was proud of the aggressive recruiting plan for minority teachers he had developed and the success he had been able to achieve in attracting new teachers to the district. The plan was based on early recruiting and hiring. Union City offered contracts to new graduates as soon after the first of the year as possible, prior to teacher resignations and retirements. New teachers were offered a general contract without specifications about grade level and location.

The only glitch in the plan was the difficulties he had trying to place the new teachers. The problem wasn't lack of positions. He had yet to estimate badly and hire too many teachers. The problem was that the principals preferred to hire people they knew from inside the school district. Because principals had the right of refusal on any new teacher, they had so far been able to defeat his efforts to place the new people.

The previous summer, several new teachers he sent out to interview with a building principal had been rejected for one of a variety of reasons: "not qualified to teach at this grade level," "lacks experience of the sort we need at this school," "overqualified for the position we have." Then, in August, just before the opening of school, the Personnel Office had been flooded with memos from principals requesting the transfer of a teacher from a school within the district to fill the same position on an emergency action. Manuel had accepted the first memo he got at face value. When the eighth such request arrived from a principal who had during the summer refused to place the new hires, he asked a personnel assistant to do some checking and discovered that the memos were part of a deliberate strategy by several principals to get people they knew on their building staffs.

This summer it had started again. He was faced with a group of twenty newly hired, primarily minority teachers and several principals who were rejecting them for a variety of reasons, none of which stood up under close examination. The court order wasn't being implemented. His recruiting plan was failing for lack of building-level cooperation, and he wasn't going to let that happen.

He picked up the phone and called Henry Harsner, a junior high school principal who had already rejected two of the new teachers that had been sent to him for an interview. Hank had done the same thing the previous summer and had eventually filled his eighth-grade science position by the transfer of an experienced teacher from a nearby school.

"Hank? This is Manuel Ortiz. Look, we have a problem here." (Pause) "Well, I hope you can help. I see that you turned down the two junior high people I sent over to interview for the open position in English." (Pause) "Yes, I can see that you reported one lacked experience with extracurricular activities and the other seemed too academic for the job. Hank, you realize that both of these teachers have very strong recommendations from their universities?" (Pause) "Hank, I hate to be arbitrary, but I'm done playing games with hiring. Unless you're willing to reconsider one of these two teachers you've interviewed, I'm telling you that you are stuck with the next person I send out who is even remotely qualified. Do you hear what I'm saying?" (Pause) "That's right. Let me know by tomorrow if you're willing to reconsider. Talk to you then."

Manuel knew he was taking a chance. If Hank refused to cooperate, Manuel wasn't sure he could force the issue without a nasty confrontation. But he was tired of letting these old guys run the show their own way.

CASE 5.10: SHOULD THE TEACHERS BE INVOLVED?

Each year for the past several years the superintendent had asked the elementary principal and the secondary principal in Evergreen Park School District to determine the items to be purchased with the district's Chapter 2 funds. The money was available through the Education Consolidation and Improvement Act (ECIA) of 1983 and required application through the State Department of Education.

In the past both principals had come up with items and together made the final determinations, even though the superintendent had suggested that they consult with the teachers. This year, however, the superintendent appointed a committee to work with the principals and to review any requests from staff. The advisory committee included Martha (Marty) Taylor, parent of an elementary student; Judith Markowitz, a third-grade teacher; and Art Van Horn, the district media specialist and high school librarian, who had volunteered to be a member of the committee. Art had a special interest in the committee. He had noticed that little money had been spent on media programs in the district since Title IV had been eliminated under the ECIA several years before. George Spooner, the new elementary school principal, and Grady Carroll, the secondary school principal, were the co-chairs.

No meetings of the committee were scheduled until mid-January. Applications from the district were due at the State Department of Education on February 1. At the first meeting of the committee, Grady was not present. He had scheduled a parent conference for the same time, and he told Art, "It's your responsibility to make sure the high school gets its fair share of the funding."

George opened the meeting by outlining the committee's task. He asked everyone to read the federal guidelines and distributed a copy to each committee member. George noted that the previous year the former elementary principal and Grady had recommended that this year's funds be spent to upgrade the social studies curriculum with maps, globes, and atlases. "All we need to do," he said, "is finalize what was recommended last year."

George showed the committee a file of year-old bids for maps, globes, and atlases and recommended that the committee accept the proposal from Acme Cartographers. That was the only company that had prepared a proposal for grades kindergarten through twelve. All the other companies had provided costs for elementary materials only.

Marty, who had been a substitute teacher for the district from time to time, noted that this project would expend all of the district's Chapter 2 allocation.

"Wait a minute," Art said. "I want to recommend that we purchase some video disk equipment for the media program."

Judith noted that no teachers had been consulted when the map bids had been solicited. She had wanted to talk to the sales representative, but no opportunity to meet with him had been provided for teachers.

George tried to get the committee back to the proposal. "I'm sure that this video disk idea is good, Art, but we really need the maps and globes. Maybe your video stuff could wait until next year. Look, I have another commitment. If you folks can meet again briefly on Friday after school, I'd like you to review the map bids and bring a recommendation to that meeting."

After George left, Marty, Judith, and Art discussed his request. They agreed that upgrading social studies materials was a high priority at both the elementary and secondary levels, but they also saw a need for video disk equipment. They decided that 80 percent of the grant dollars should be spent for maps, globes, and atlases and the other 20 percent should be used to begin purchasing video disk materials. They also decided that classroom teachers should determine which maps were most needed rather than their depending on company salespeople. Judith volunteered to ask George to call the salesperson from Acme who had prepared the bid and ask if a company representative could visit the school and update the proposal using information from the teachers.

Marty, Judith, and Art were the only ones present at the meeting on Friday after school. Judith reported that she had talked with George concerning the decisions made after he had left the meeting on Wednesday. He was not pleased. He had told her that Art had "messed up the process" by requesting the video disk equipment. "Obviously," George had said, "the decision should have been made; the committee should have just accepted the Acme proposal."

Because George had seemed so upset, Judith had called the Acme sales representative herself and arranged for a visit to the school district the following Monday. When she told George that on Thursday, he had not reacted much, just said that he supposed it wouldn't hurt to update the old proposal. He had, however, told Judith that he wouldn't be able to attend the meeting on Friday. Because he had believed that the task had been finished before he left the meeting on Wednesday, he had made another commitment.

Art, Marty, and Judith weren't quite sure what to do. Judith, who was becoming defensive about the process, noted that the group had done exactly what George had asked, reviewed the bid and made recommendations. "He didn't tell us," she said, "that it had to come out the way he planned it."

As they talked over their concerns, they noticed that Grady walked past the room twice. He never acknowledged that he saw them, but they were sure that he did. Finally, the three of them decided that they would schedule one more meeting, after school the following Wednesday, and send notices to George and Grady. Judith also recommended that all three of them try to see the sales representative on Monday. "That way," she said, "we'll be ready to make a decision on Wednesday."

Judith, Marty, and Art were the only ones present at the meeting the next Wednesday. The Acme sales representative had visited the district as promised on Monday, but he had not spent any time talking to teachers about their needs. Judith had noticed him waiting to see George and had asked the office secretary to schedule an appointment for her during her planning time, but she was told that the representative would not be available then.

Marty said that she was very concerned about the lack of administrative involvement in the committee. Judith explained that she had made sure that George was informed about the committee's meetings and the decision that had been made. Art agreed that the administrators should have been involved, but he pointed out that they had received notices about the meetings just as the rest of them had. They had chosen not to attend. Marty suggested that the group call the superintendent and share their concerns with him. They tried, but he was not in the office. Marty offered to contact him and speak to him as a member of the committee and a concerned parent. All three agreed to meet again the next day after school.

As Art walked to the meeting the next day, he met Marty. She stayed only long enough to say that she had talked to the superintendent at home the night before and that he had said he would look into the matter. George had called her at noon and told her that it wouldn't be necessary for her to attend today's meeting, but she had wanted to make sure that the committee members knew she had talked to the superintendent. With that, she left.

George was the only committee member in the room when Art

arrived. Marty, he said, would not be at the meeting. Judith was attending a special education staffing, and he also was supposed to be at that meeting. He would be brief. George told Art that the request for funds for the State Department of Education was nearly complete and that it would be submitted on time.

"What are you requesting?" Art asked.

"We are proposing to spend 70 percent of the allocation on social studies materials, 10 percent on video disk equipment, and 20 percent on computers. Thanks for your help. The committee won't need to meet again. Now I have to go to the staffing."

Art sat in the room by himself, the only remaining member of the advisory committee on the allocation of Chapter 2 funds.

CASE 5.11: THE REQUEST TO SHARE RESOURCES

Under state board of education rules, school districts are permitted to contract outside the district for up to and including 90 of the 390 course units required for graduation. If they exceed that amount, the state will not accredit the district. Two superintendents—Brian McGlaughlin, superintendent of the Deer Run Community District, and Malcolm Everett, superintendent of the Hurley Community School District—are discussing the arguments they will use to request waiver of this rule when they appear before the state board. Deer Run District enrolls 70 students in grades seven through twelve. Hurley Community District has 50 students in grades seven through twelve. The districts are about ten miles apart and are connected by a paved county road.

"Then we agree that we want to maintain our elementary schools?" said Brian McGlaughlin, the Deer Run superintendent.

"Yes," agreed Malcolm Everett of Hurley. "Community members from both our districts have made it clear that it is essential to keep the neighborhood school for our elementary-age youngsters."

"In fact," said McGlaughlin, "if the board asks us why we don't request to take the next step and consolidate the two districts, community desire to maintain separate elementary programs can be our major argument. You and I both know that not everyone supports the notion of our sharing resources, so keeping our elementary schools is one way to counter those who are concerned about losing community identity. Tell me, what other questions do you think we should be prepared for, Malcolm?"

"Well, Brian, though the reasons are clear to us, someone on the state board is certain to ask why we have proposed that our districts share staff, programs, and students. When that question comes, I think that we should respond by talking about more efficient use of teachers, expansion of curricular offerings, and less duplication of services."

"Those are the most obvious categories for us to address. But we also need to give some specific examples to support our arguments. We should tell them what courses we'll be able to add to our program if the board approves our request."

"We'll just tell them what was reported in the recent study by the Deer Run-Hurley Joint Planning Committee. The committee suggested that we could offer French, advanced Spanish, advanced biology, astronomy, and conservation at the high school level. It proposed four additional nine-week courses for the junior high school, including computer keyboarding and industrial arts."

Brian McGlaughlin nodded his head in agreement. He could see the presentation shaping up in his own mind; there were, however, several loose ends to consider. Athletics might well be the greatest stumbling block for their plan. The board might also be concerned about the logistics of moving students between the two communities. He shared both of these concerns with Everett.

After a lengthy silence, Malcolm Everett spoke, "You and I both know how important competitive athletics has been in our communities over the years. I think we can deal with this issue by arguing that we will only be continuing what we are already doing. We need to tell them that currently we're carrying out successful sports programs at the junior high level by combining students from both districts. When students enter high school, they play for their home district. We haven't had any complaints or problems with this arrangement from parents, and the kids certainly have handled it well. On the other hand, the level of performance would undoubtedly be raised if we used this opportunity to merge the high school teams. Some other school districts in the country are trying that arrangement."

"I wasn't aware of that, Malcolm," said Brian. "A great many people here who are already concerned about community identity might see an arrangement such as that as a serious threat to their notion of what community means. I'm reluctant to go that far with our proposal."

"On the matter of logistics, we can simply report what the joint planning committee recommended. Senior high school students and some teachers from Deer Run would be transported to Hurley for afternoon classes, while junior high school students from Hurley would be taken to Deer Run. The planning committee didn't address the issue of how the costs of transportation would be covered. That is something we'll need to deal with if and when our request to the state board is approved."

Malcolm Everett was feeling better. The hard work was paying off, and they would present a tight proposal for resource sharing to the board. "Sounds great, Brian," he said. "Just one more matter. How do we respond if someone asks us whether we will obtain greater efficiency at the expense of the teachers in the two districts? How will our plan affect current employees? Will we release any teachers?"

"My suggestion is that we simply say that we hope to avoid releasing any teachers. We won't replace faculty or staff who retire or resign, provided, of course, that those leaving are in areas that are overstaffed when the two districts begin sharing programs. For example, my guidance counselor has just turned in his resignation, effective at the end of this school year. I suspect that we'll be able to work out an arrangement that will permit your guidance counselor to serve both districts."

"I think we've done about as much as we can to prepare for our meeting with the state board," said Brian. "It seems to me that we've covered all the bases. We'll just have to see if we have anticipated the issues and concerns the board will raise. Regardless, I'm satisfied that we have come up with a plan that will provide quality education for our young people."

"I couldn't agree more," responded Malcolm. "See you at the state board meeting next week. In the meantime, let me know if any new information comes to light. We've finished our meeting ahead of schedule, and I think I'll take the back roads over to my office and mull over our discussion. If I come up with any additional ideas, I'll be in touch."

CASE 5.12: USING THE LOTTERY TO FINANCE EDUCATION

"Good to see you here, Jack," Superintendent of Schools Frank Howard said to Jack Kroeger, editor of the Rosehill *Daily Record*.

"I try to attend most of the Chamber of Commerce meetings, Frank, but I did miss the last several."

"Printed any good news lately?"

"Well, I don't really think about news as good or not. You folks in education must think that the state lottery is pretty good news, though. We've run several stories about how sales have exceeded expectations."

"Jack, lottery sales are higher than expected, but the lottery itself hasn't produced the new money for education that we expected. Several people I've talked to have made a faulty assumption: high sales mean less need for taxes. The legislators have made the same mistake and have made decisions which, in effect, use the lottery revenues to replace education dollars that had been provided from other state tax sources prior to the lottery."

"If that's what's happening, people ought to know about it. I thought the purpose of the lottery was to make more money available for new educational programs. We certainly need it."

"Sure we do. Part of the problem, of course, is that our student enrollments are growing so fast. It's hard to make people understand that all the hoopla about the lottery has resulted in education getting less rather than more dollars per pupil."

"How about writing a guest editorial for the *Daily Record* about this?"

"An editorial is probably a good idea. If it appears under my name, though, it will seem self-serving. I'd be glad to draft something, Jack, but I'd prefer that you print it as yours."

"That's a deal."

Three days later, the following editorial appeared in the Rosehill *Daily Record*:

Lottery Boom a Bust for Education

An extremely small percentage of our state residents are getting rich from the state lottery, but the large number of public school students who had hoped to benefit are not even breaking even.

Given what the Legislature appropriated for education in the 1980s, the amount for the current fiscal year certainly should have been higher than it turned out to be. The amount budgeted included a full year of lottery revenue; that is an indication that the lottery has been used to replace education dollars.

It is not necessarily that legislators are consciously cheating. They are allocating the 35 percent of the funds that were to be put in trust for education to the support of schools. But the usual money appropriated for education is not keeping up with the combined effects of inflation and the increasing student population.

The lottery began producing money in midyear of the last fiscal year. State spending should have increased to $3,114 for each student from regular appropriations, adjusted for inflation, based on the growth trend of the 1980s. The actual figure was $2,996, with lottery funds included.

This year, the amount per student should have been $3,217, without lottery funds. With lottery funds, it will be $3,201 (at the current inflation rate). These numbers indicate that the additional lottery money has pulled education back up almost to where it would have been financially without the lottery if the Legislature had continued its spending pattern.

These are likely to be the best years of the lottery. Typically, interest falls off in state lotteries and the legislative neglect increases amid a feeling of complacency and the attitude that "education has been taken care of" by the lottery. Other states have had to increase the amount of revenue returned as prizes in order to sustain interest. Several states have gone to regional lotteries.

In our state, half the money goes back to the players. Another 15

> percent is spent on overhead. The rest goes into education, about $323 million this past year. But that was only 3.9 percent of the education budget in the state, and it replaced money the Legislature would have spent and should have spent without the lottery.
>
> The lottery has turned out to be a bad bet for education. It has, in fact, served mainly as a mask for a reduction in public commitment toward education.

Frank read the editorial with some pride. It presented the issues succinctly, was factual, and would be persuasive, he thought, for anyone who took the time to read it. As superintendent of schools, Frank planned to contact as many influential community members as possible and poll them about their reactions to the editorial. That would give him a chance to answer their questions and reinforce the message. He wondered what else he could do to lobby for reform of the lottery. Should he now write a letter to the editor of the *Daily Record* in support of the editorial he had written anonymously?

CASE 5.13: RENOVATING THE SCHOOL OF THE ARTS

Superintendent of Schools Donald Sharpe sat alone in his office prior to the monthly meeting of the Kingston County Board of Education. Sharpe was thinking about his recent relations with the Board of Education. "Acrimonious" was the word a friend of his had used. It probably fit. For 11 years he had not wavered in his commitment to improving the academic standards of the schools and to bringing national recognition to the school district. Some characterized his manner as akin to that of a Baptist preacher, a label he accepted with pride. He knew he had made a difference, but in recent years the same approaches that had first brought him plaudits seemed to be the target of growing opposition.

Attempts to oust his opponents on the board had failed in the school board election two months earlier. During the first board meeting following the election, Zoe Millan, president of the teachers' association, had expressed the teachers' dissatisfaction with the superintendent's leadership. Sharpe had 18 months left in his contract, and neither the teachers' association nor the school board could identify any cause for terminating his contract. Yet, the teachers had called for his resignation, and board members had asked him to accept an alternative assignment with the district at the same salary. He responded that he had been hired to be superintendent and that he intended to fulfill that commitment. He felt that was the right thing to do, though he knew there was no chance the contract would be extended and that he would be dealing with strong opposition on the board for the remainder of his contract term.

Toward the end of the meeting, Board President Fritz Hess had announced his intention to step down, after several years as president, because of ill health. Hess recommended that Vice-President Stuart Ervey be named president. That recommendation was supported by the other two opposition members, Russell Dunn and Billie Jean Hartman. Only Jill Varner, Bryan McCalley, and Willie Kennis had voted against it. In other words, the vote had been typical of every vote in recent months: 4 to 3 against the superintendent.

Tonight he knew that the 4–3 split would affect discussion of the Stephen Foster School of the Arts. The question that would come before the board was whether to put money into the school at its present location or to move it to a school a mile away with low enrollment. Both proposals would be costly ventures. He knew that the vote would go against him. He just didn't know how.

Case 5.13: Part II

As always, Ervey took too much time with the ceremonies and preliminaries at the beginning of the agenda. When the board finally reached the agenda item concerning the School of the Arts, Ervey spent some time reviewing prior discussions of the issues. He concluded with a summary: "In view of the fact that this is a large building program and that it has been delayed for several months, it is time to make a decision. As I see it, the board has three choices: spend money to enhance the school at its present location; move it to Sherman Junior High School, a school that would require substantial renovation; or move it to some unnamed location."

Billie Jean Hartman began: "The superintendent has recommended that we spend $9.9 million dollars to renovate Sherman Junior High and relocate the Stephen Foster School to the Sherman location. I'm against it. I move that we change the dollar amount to $5.6 million and keep the school where it is."

Hess seconded her motion.

Ervey opened the discussion: "When the renovation of Sherman was first discussed, I was in favor of it. Moving the School of the Arts to that location would permit the present school building to serve neighborhood children and would ensure that Sherman's enrollment would be sufficient to keep it operating. There are members of the board, including me, who now have serious doubts about that proposal. Before we leave here tonight, I want some support for the location and the dollars."

Reverend Willie Kennis spoke next: "It seems to me we're acting a little bit hasty here. Where does the recommendation to spend $5.6 million come from? We don't have any information about what you can do with $3.5 million, what you can do with $4 million or with $5 million. We're playing with numbers unless we know what the need is, what the minimum requirement is to develop the school."

Bryan McCalley supported Kennis. "I share your concern, Reverend Kennis. We do not have a recommendation from the Facilities Department for this dollar amount. If we reject their recommendation for $9.9 million, I think we should give them a chance to come back to us with a new recommendation."

Dunn had a suggestion. "We might proceed in this way. We could set the amount and have the Facilities Department bring back to us for approval what they could do with that amount. That would at least give the citizens something to hold on to and . . . ."

Reverend Kennis interrupted: "Let me clarify what I tried to say a minute ago. The Facilities Division at one time had a plan for $3.5 million. We have no plan for the $5.6 million we have on the table now. I'm just wondering what was deficient in the $3.5 million dollar plan that would require an additional $2 million. That still isn't enough to build an auditorium, for example."

Ervey recognized Dunn. "There is an approach where you designate the dollar amount you have to work with, and then you design accordingly. Why not take that approach? You might want a Cadillac, but you can't have a tape deck and all that in it."

Hess slammed his agenda notebook closed. "I'm going to support this motion. The principle is the same as the one we operate with on our total school budget. We set the amount of money. I like what Mr. Dunn said. I think we ought to vote on it."

Reverend Kennis indicated he wanted to speak. "We need to get on the record how people vote on this. We need to see who's for it, and who's against it."

Hartman turned toward Reverend Kennis. "No one's against any-thing, Reverend Kennis. We just need to anticipate what the taxpayers of this community will support."

"Are you ready to vote?" Ervey asked. "The motion is that $5.6 million be allocated to renovate the Stephen Foster School of the Arts at its present location. All those in favor?" Hess, Hartman, Dunn, and Ervey raised their hands.

"Against?" Varner, McCalley, and Kennis raised their hands.

"The ayes have it, four to three. Now what's going to happen is that the superintendent will bring back to us a schedule for what we can get with this amount of money. Next item."

Superintendent Sharpe's fears had been confirmed. The board had no idea what $5.6 would provide for the school or for children in the district.

They had voted against his recommendation, and that was enough. He felt his 11 years with the district coming to an end. He wished that he had more options. He could look for another job, but resigning his position in Kingston County would mean that his opponents on the board had won. He had decided that wouldn't happen. He could continue to do his job and hope that over time he would be able to rebuild his support among the teachers and in the community. He wasn't sure that was possible. All he was sure of was that he wasn't going to let Stuart Ervey and his cronies get the best of him.

CASE 5.14: WHAT THE PUBLIC THINKS IS IMPORTANT

Superintendent of Schools Jacob Holmes had appointed the long-range planning committee several weeks earlier. The committee included representatives from area businesses, influential members of minority groups, parents, teachers, and administrators. Holmes's intent was to have the committee examine the future needs of the district and develop ways to nurture community support for those needs. At the first meeting of the committee, Superintendent Holmes described the committee's charge and appointed a subcommittee to look at marketing issues.

During the second meeting, the superintendent presented information about current conditions in the Normandy School District. His presentation included several tables. Table 1 listed the age and type of school buildings in the district.

Table 2 showed that a declining percentage of the budget had been spent on maintenance. During the same time, operations expenses had been fairly constant.

TABLE 1: AGE AND TYPE OF SCHOOL BUILDINGS

Type of Unit		Original Building	
Facility	Number	Date	Number
Senior high	8		7
Junior high	13	Before 1900	18
Elementary	64[a]	1900–1919	17[b]
Special education	1	1920–1939	12
Other	1	1940–1959	31
		1960–1979	2
		1980–present	
Total	**87**	**Total**	**87**

[a] Includes one closed building.
[b] Includes two closed buildings.

TABLE 2: PERCENTAGE OF EXPENDITURES BY FUNCTION

Function	4 Years Ago	3 Years Ago	2 Years Ago	Last Year
General administration	2.51	2.39	2.24	2.54
Instruction	71.40	71.64	72.07	71.59
Support services	2.25	2.02	2.09	2.17
Transportation	5.21	5.97	5.91	6.16
Operation	11.45	12.11	11.87	12.24
Fixed charges	1.31	.49	.38	.36
Maintenance	5.15	4.67	4.35	3.82
Tax collection fees	.68	.67	.56	.60
Other	.04	.04	.53	.52
Total	**100.00**	**100.00**	**100.00**	**100.00**

The final table, Table 3, showed that site and building fund expenditures also had declined over a four-year period.

TABLE 3: SITE AND BUILDING FUND EXPENDITURES

Purpose	4 Years Ago	3 Years Ago	2 Years Ago	Last Year
Site	$ 93,658	596,000	$ 296,000	$ 38,786
Improvements	730,461	1,543,181	383,159	322,879
New buildings	6,311,766	3,301,369	3,050,256	2,582,200
Equipment for buildings	111,098	100,631	170,900	131,955
Tax collection	20,430	21,869	21,742	28,589
Total	**$7,267,413**	**$5,563,050**	**$3,922,057**	**$3,104,409**

Superintendent Holmes noted that during the same period school enrollments had been steady. The effect, he concluded, was that several school buildings and school sites in the Normandy School District were in desperate condition and needed attention immediately.

"There is absolutely no way the district can remodel, update, and improve the overall physical plants without increasing taxes," he noted. "There is no doubt we need some major work done on these facilities. In the past, increases in the school district taxes have gone for salaries and fringe benefits. We're now at a point where we either pay now or pay later for these renovations."

"My understanding is that you are asking for a big increase," said Mary Anne Noble, president of the League of Women Voters. "If I recall correctly, district building needs were estimated at about 30 million dollars two years ago. The estimate I've heard lately is 112 million dollars. That's quite a change. I'm not at all sure that taxpayers in this community will support this."

"My conviction is that people will support what they can see is needed," the superintendent responded. "The need is clear. We can show it on paper. People can see it when they drive by the buildings or walk into the classrooms. Citizens will support a comprehensive, defensible plan for building and renovation because they want their children to go to schools that are safe, clean, and attractive."

Several members of the long-range planning group indicated that they weren't as convinced as the superintendent of schools. One member noted that fewer and fewer households in the school district contained school-age children. Another remarked that it was her understanding that private and parochial school enrollments had been growing in recent years and that several new Christian schools had opened in the community.

Carlos Ruiz, chairman of the marketing subcommittee, suggested that his subcommittee might have some data by the next meeting that would help the group get a clearer, more exact picture of community sentiments. "We have employed two consultants from our local university who have helped us develop a survey of the community on several issues. Telephone interviews will be conducted at the end of the month. We should be able to report back to you at our next meeting."

Superintendent Holmes was visibly surprised, but he covered it well. "I hadn't realized you were going to move quite so quickly, Carlos."

"No reason to delay, Jake. We need to know what the people think."

"Can you give us a couple of weeks before you start the interviews?"

"I'm sure we can," Carlos replied. "Why?"

"We're ready to release the results of our consultant's study of school facilities," Holmes responded. "The study supports the needs I've outlined for you here today. We want to release the information to the public as a kind of trial balloon to see what support is out there."

"That shouldn't be any problem," Carlos replied. "People's opinions are unlikely to be affected by a couple of articles in the newspapers and a television newscast, but we can easily wait until you've released the information you want to get out there."

During the next few weeks the district released portions of the facilities study and statements by the superintendent and several school board members. Response from the public was limited and negative. The following letters to the editor of the local paper were published.

Property tax unfair

As a property owner, I am tired of carrying the load for others. Three-quarters of my taxes go to schools. Many people pay little or nothing to educate their children, while others pay many times their fair share. Common sense tells us that using property taxes to fund schools is extremely unfair.

When is the Legislature going to wake up to the fact that property taxes are regressive? If you keep your place in good shape, your taxes go up. The railroads revolted against unfair taxes, and yet our school tax is even more unfair. It's time for property owners to revolt.

Normandy Taxpayer

School Plan Appalling

The multi-million dollar school renovation plan is appalling. Why have the superintendent and his administration just now realized a need for all the renovation and expansion? What have they been doing in the past? The big push the past few years has been for higher pay and better benefits for educators. Why have the needs of the physical facilities been ignored?

Superintendent Holmes states that the improvements must be done and there is "absolutely no way" they can be done without increasing taxes. Taxpayers apparently have nothing to say in the matter.

An Angry Taxpayer

Soon after the district released the information about the building needs and possible plans for construction, a local telemarketing firm surveyed 600 randomly selected parents of children in the Normandy Public Schools and 600 randomly selected citizens without children in the same district.

At the third meeting of the long-range planning committee, Carlos Ruiz was ready with a report on the marketing survey. In general, he said, people feel that the quality of education provided by the Normandy Public Schools is high. Over 60 percent of the parents and 55 percent of other community members graded the schools with an "A" or a "B." That compared very favorably with national surveys of public opinions about the public schools.

That general satisfaction carried over into satisfaction with many specific aspects of the schools and school programs, Carlos said. "Of particular interest to us is the fact that 73 percent of the parents and 70 percent of other community members believe that too much or enough is being spent on care of school buildings. Citizens don't recognize the needs as Superintendent Holmes outlined them to us last month. They feel that the schools are in pretty good shape."

"But that's simply not true," the superintendent responded. "The data we have collected and the consultant's recommendations show clear needs for more maintenance, for renovation, and for new buildings."

"Jake," Carlos replied, "you won't like what I'm going to say, but it really doesn't matter what's true. What's important is what people believe. If you're going to recommend a tax increase or ask people to support the issuance of bonds for construction, you'll have to help them to see the problem as you do."

After a lengthy and awkward silence, the superintendent said, "You may be right. What does the committee suggest that we do?"

CHAPTER 6

Managing External Politics

For those systems that escape or are spared the ravages of internal conflict, it is even more remarkable that . . . they have not foundered on the sharp and more dangerous shoals located in the total environment of the system.

David Easton

CASE 6.1: REQUIRING THE PARENTS TO GO TO SCHOOL

Several parents were in the audience as the Lester County School Board meeting opened. During the time set aside for constituents to address the board, Malcolm Skolow, parent of a senior at Lester County Senior High School, rose to speak.

"The recent decision of the principal at Lester County High School to punish both students involved in the party at Green Springs Inlet and their parents is absolutely arbitrary and totally unfair," Mr. Skolow began. "The principal acted on hearsay evidence. Innocent students and parents have been hurt."

Dr. Jasper Powell, president of the school board, looked at the superintendent of schools. Superintendent MacDowell leaned over and spoke briefly with the associate superintendent, then responded to Powell's unasked question. "In early October, 19 seniors and 10 juniors at Lester High School were absent in the morning. Principal Dwayne Wallace had

103

heard from one of the assistant principals that there was reason to suspect that most of those students were at a party at the edge of town, Green Springs Inlet, as Mr. Skolow suggested. The principal called the sheriff's department, and the sheriff's youth unit investigated the incident. They reported that 60 cans of beer had been consumed before 11:00 A.M. Deputies charged one person with serving alcohol to minors.

"Board members will recall," the superintendent continued, "that school board policy stipulates that if students are caught attending a party or other function where drugs or alcohol are being used, they face either a three-day out-of-school suspension and counseling sessions that they and their parents must attend twice a week for six weeks, or a ten-day out-of-school suspension. In this case, the principal choose the three-day suspension and counseling."

Board member Jane Garvey raised her hand. "Has this policy been used in the past?"

"Yes," Superintendent MacDowell replied, "the policy has been used several times during the past two years. I believe, however, that this is the first time that the three-day option has been used."

Mr. Skolow, who had been standing at the podium during this exchange, indicated that he wished to speak. "Several of us wish to speak on this issue. Let me just say that my daughter didn't even go into the house where the party was held. It's unfair to make her attend counseling, and it is certainly unfair to make me attend counseling. I yield the floor to Mrs. Judy Pearson."

As Mr. Skolow took his seat in the audience, Mrs. Pearson walked to the podium. "I, too, am upset about how the school administrators have handled the punishment process. I feel as though my son is being held hostage. The school principal has committed me to a class, and no one ever asked me. I yield the floor to Reverend Douglas Husome."

Reverend Husome searched his pocket for a slip of notepaper as he walked to the podium. "No one has been more supportive of this school district than I have . . . until now. My daughter Leslie told me that she didn't drink at the party. I believe her. The one thing that dominates this whole event is unfairness to the children and to the parents. My daughter has been branded as an alcohol abuser, and she doesn't drink and I don't drink. Where's the justice in that? What's the lesson for our children?"

Three other parents took the podium to give their positions. All reported that their children had told them that they either had not had a drink or had left the party when they found out that beer was being served. When the parents finished, board member Garvey addressed the board. "I move we show our support for the principal's decision. We will send a message to the community about drinking."

Board member Wallace Egan seconded her motion, adding his own comments. "As you know, I have proposed that we expel students caught with alcohol and drugs on campus. We need to take a tough stand on this. It may seem unfair to punish some children who say they weren't drinking, but these kids were out of school and they weren't over at Green Springs Inlet studying."

In the vote that followed, the board unanimously voted to support the decision of the principal.

After the board meeting, Principal Wallace was interviewed by a reporter from the local newspaper. In his remarks, he defended his decision. "Had the students been in school, we wouldn't be here tonight at this board meeting. None of these students is known as a problem drinker. They were just doing dumb kids' things. I think that incidents such as this help parents realize that even good kids need parents checking up on them."

When asked by the reporter how he justified requiring classes of the parents, Wallace replied, "We can't control what students do during off-school hours. We must work with parents because we have to do something to educate them and help them organize networks of parents who will support each other in prohibiting the use of alcohol and drugs in their homes. We're not trying to be punitive. I'm sorry that some parents have chosen to see it that way, but at least we got their attention."

Though he had spoken with confidence to the reporter, Dwayne Wallace had his own doubts as he scraped the frost from his windshield. He wondered what he or the superintendent or the board would do if parents flat out refused to attend the class, and he knew that was very possible.

CASE 6.2: THE CHAMBER WITHDRAWS SUPPORT

Superintendent of Schools Jeffrey Johnson passed around copies of the recent letter to the editor from Dale Richardson, executive director of the Madison Chamber of Commerce, for members of the administrative team to read. In his letter, Richardson had stated that his organization would no longer be able to support increases in the school budget that require an increase in the property tax rate. Several influential local businesses, according to the letter, would seriously consider relocation if property taxes continued to rise.

"You'll note," Superintendent Johnson began, "that the letter implies that the Chamber has widespread community support for its position. I should also tell you that Richardson telephoned me early this morning and has informed me that he intends to present the Chamber's position before the Board of Education at its next meeting."

"I'm really sorry I missed the last meeting of the Education Committee of the Chamber," said Julius Glazer, assistant superintendent for business and finance. "I might have been able to head this off, but I was at a conference in Chicago the last time they met. I had no idea that this was coming, I'm sorry to say."

"Julius, how much do the members of the Education Committee, members of the Chamber's Executive Committee, or Chamber members in general, for that matter, understand about the school district's needs and the recent cutbacks in state funding?" asked Martha Gresham, assistant superintendent for curriculum and instruction.

"Their interest is sincere," Glazer replied. "Several members have a pretty good understanding of the state finance formula, and most of them understand the limitations of the tax base in the state. The problem is that they are even more aware of the recent threats by major businesses in the community to relocate, and the Chamber's efforts to recruit new businesses into the community have not been very successful. The letter may be a grandstand play more than an honest reflection of what Richardson and other Chamber members really believe."

"My question," began Claude Martin, assistant superintendent for personnel and community relations, "is whether we should just let Richardson address the Board of Education and see what happens or whether we should try to prevent that?"

"I'm not sure about that either," Johnson began. "I think I should try talking to Richardson informally, off the record, to learn what I can about how widespread and serious the support is for the sentiments in this letter."

"If you do that," said Glazer, "the rest of us could get on the phone with other members of the Chamber's Executive Committee and Education Committee to see what we can learn."

"That's a pretty good idea," responded Johnson. "I just think it's important that we don't appear to circumvent Richardson. Just as I would not want the Chamber representatives to visit with individual members of the school board without talking to me, I think Richardson should be contacted before we try to influence his Executive Committee. After I've talked to him, it's 'open season' and we can go to the Executive Committee."

"I'm still concerned," said Gresham, "about how much people really understand. Do they know about the recent cuts in state aid? Do they understand our increased costs because of state-mandated programs? They may understand the tax base, but I'm concerned that they don't understand what we need in order to provide legal and quality education for children in this city."

"Most of this has been discussed in the Education Committee,"

Glazer responded, "but I don't think the Executive Committee has talked about it much. That's where the problem may be."

"I'm really sorry we're in this position," Johnson said. "I'd rather act than react, and we seem to have lost the initiative here. I'd prefer to be on top of things. This never should have happened. Now that it has, we have to respond in a way that gives us the edge."

Martha Gresham tried to turn the conversation to a different aspect of the problem. "Jeff, do you think you should be the one who talks to Richardson, or should we ask the president of the school board to represent us?"

"Now don't take this personally, Martha," Julius Glazer replied, "but if Howard Simpson were still president of the board I'd strongly recommend that we ask him to represent the school district. He had strong ties to the business community. But now that Mary Jane Hanson is board president, I think the superintendent should be the district's representative."

"I assume you think she'd be ineffective because she's a woman," Martha said testily. "I can't believe you'd really say that."

"Look, Martha, I admit that Mary Jane is one of the strongest advocates for education ever elected to the board, but I just don't think a former teacher, now housewife, would have much credibility with the Chamber of Commerce," Julius said, defending himself.

"I'm less concerned about who talks to Richardson than I am about what we say," said Claude Martin.

"Let me try to summarize," replied Jeff. "We explain why our costs have increased. We remind them of the tax situation in this state, referring them to their own study of the erosion of the tax base in recent years. We point out that education is still the best bargain in town."

"What if they still think that school costs are too high?" Martin asked.

"Then I think we need to get them involved," Jeff replied. "I think we need to throw it back to them and ask where they would suggest cutting programs and expenses. Then they would realize that once you begin cutting programs, every program is important. We should get those businesspeople who will not support us to share in the responsibility. How do we explain to 300 parents and students that a given program they think is important will no longer be available? I'd like someone from the Chamber to tell me how to do that?"

Julius Glazer shifted in his chair. "That strategy may work, but I think it's important to avoid the impression that we're starting a fight with Richardson or the Chamber."

"It's apparent to me," Claude Martin interjected, "that it's the

Chamber that's initiating the fight, not the school district. They may not think that, but they are."

"Whoever may have started it," Jeff replied, "if we fight with them, we're in a no-win situation for the students in this school district. We can't let that happen."

"I certainly agree with that," Martha said. "The problem is that we know our situation better than they do. Probably half of them don't know how our tax base is calculated or how recent legislative decisions to remove some classes of industrial and agricultural property from the state property tax base have affected the funding of schools. I guess what that really means is that we have an additional obligation, the obligation of educating the taxpayers about school funding."

"That's right," Jeff said. "We need to show them where the dollars come from, where the dollars go, who the dollars affect, and what cutting dollars would do. If no one has an objection, I'm going to call Mary Jane this afternoon, give her the information we have, and suggest that I meet with Richardson as soon as possible. We have to do everything we can to head off a public confrontation between the Board of Education and the Chamber of Commerce."

CASE 6.3: THE PRAYER GROUP
AT HORACE MANN HIGH SCHOOL

Alan Strickland walked into Principal Darla Smithe's office. He had the easy, confident walk of a senior about to graduate from high school. Alan had not had a distinguished academic career at Horace Mann High School, but he was a good student, an easy kid to work with. He came from a Catholic family in the community, but his parents had divorced a few years before. The change had been tough on Alan. The previous year he had not been at Horace Mann but had instead attended Word of Life Christian Academy in a neighboring community. Darla had noticed that Alan now spent most of his social time with a particular group of students, most of whom appeared to share fundamentalist Christian convictions.

"What can I do for you, Alan?" Darla began.

"I came in to ask you if I can get a group of students together to talk about the Bible."

"I have no problem with that. In fact, you can do that any time you want."

"You don't understand. We want to have a room in the school and a school sponsor," Alan explained.

"That's a bit different. That would be against school board policy. Our policy says that a school-sponsored group should have a faculty supervisor and should not be supported by, I'm quoting now, 'any religious or political group or by any organization that denies membership on the basis of race, creed, gender, or political belief.' That pretty much rules out the kind of formal sponsorship you are asking for. You know, Southside Community Church is right next door. I'd be glad to call the church to arrange for you to meet there. I'm sure they wouldn't mind."

"We don't want to meet at the church, Mrs. Smithe. We want to meet at the high school. If that is your final answer to my request, I would like to meet with the superintendent."

"Let me think about this, Alan. I'll get back to you with an answer tomorrow."

When Alan left, Darla called both Superintendent of Schools Craig Middelstadt and the associate superintendent, Julie Feldhausen. Both of them agreed with her interpretation that the board policy would prohibit providing school sponsorship for a Christian study group. Dr. Feldhausen said that she would verify the position with the school lawyer and suggested that she, the superintendent, and Darla meet the next day to talk over the situation.

"I'd like that," Darla had told her. "I have a feeling that we're being set up."

The next day Darla made a point of talking to Alan before her meeting with the superintendent and associate superintendent. She told him that she could not approve the request. His only response had been, "Who do I talk to next?"

At her meeting with Dr. Middelstadt and Dr. Feldhausen, Dr. Feldhausen reported that the school district's lawyer had concurred with their interpretation of the board policy on student groups. The 1984 Equal Access Act, he had noted, had made it unlawful for any public secondary school that created an open forum to deny access to student-initiated groups on the basis of the religious, political, or philosophical content of the groups' speech. The law stipulates that a school has created a limited open forum when it allows one or more student groups that are not related to the curriculum to meet on school premises outside of instructional time. Thus, if a district permits any student group not directly related to school course work to meet, it must allow all student clubs to meet in the school, including religious clubs.

The school district, the lawyer argued, had not created an open forum because all of the school-sponsored clubs at Horace Mann are an integral part of the school's curriculum, are under the direct control of the school administration, and have faculty sponsors. He had used the chess club and the business clubs as examples, extensions, he said, of the school's logic course in the case of the chess club and of its business and economics courses in the case of the business club.

While Darla understood the lawyer's argument, she wasn't as confident as he seemed that she could relate each club at Horace Mann to a curriculum offering. She hoped she wouldn't have to. She told the superintendent and the associate superintendent about her conversation with Alan earlier in the day. When he had asked about the next person he should talk to, she had recommended Dr. Feldhausen. She told Julie she thought Alan would call very soon.

Two days later Julie Feldhausen called Darla to tell her that she had just finished meeting with Alan Strickland. "You're probably right, Darla," Julie had said. "We are being used as a test case. I expect this one to go all the way: hearing before the board and then a court hearing. I suspect they selected our district because they guessed that we would be willing to take the case to court. When I met with Alan, he didn't seem at all surprised by my denial of his request. He let slip in our conversation that his group is working with Kent Baxter, you know, the local lawyer who has represented several fundamentalist groups in the area in a variety of appeals. He's also a member of the Word of Life Christian Church."

As Darla hung up the phone, she thought about what lay ahead. She hoped the board would back her. She had no reason to doubt that they would, but one could never be absolutely sure. She hoped she wouldn't have to testify in court. She knew how lawyers could twist things, and she didn't look forward to having to defend herself for simply following a board policy that she also happened to believe was right.

CASE 6.4: "I CAN SEE EVIL"

Rachel Beals, the most recently elected member of the Druid Hill Community Schools Board of Education, walked into the office of Meredith Wickman, principal at Bryan Elementary School. Meredith had known that this encounter was inevitable from the time that Mrs. Beals was elected. She had promised in her campaign to visit each school in the district, to examine the school curricula, and to ensure, she said, that children were being taught appropriate values. She did not make it known during the campaign that her own children, who had once been students in the Druid Hill district, were now attending Bethel Christian Academy in a neighboring town.

Though Meredith had seen pictures of Mrs. Beals on television and in the newspapers, she was not really prepared for the petite, delicate-looking, really beautiful woman who walked through the office door. She was soft-spoken and polite as she opened the conversation. "I'm glad to meet you, Mrs. Wickman. I'm just here to tell you about my concerns. My intent is to change the curriculum in the schools. I think you should know that."

"I'm not really familiar with your concerns, Mrs. Beals, though I understand that you have a strong interest in curriculum."

"I want you to know that I am horrified by what our children are reading. One of my concerns is that our children are not reading meaningful sentences in spelling and English."

"I'm not sure what you mean by 'meaningful sentences,' Mrs. Beals."

"There were no sentences about God and Christian values in the books my own children used. You know, the words 'Christmas' and 'Easter' were not even mentioned in my second grader's books. That's one of the reasons I took my own children out of the Druid Hill schools and put them in a school where they would be taught values."

"If you are talking about religious values, we believe that is the responsibility of parents."

"Our children are being robbed of religious freedom because we don't offer them religion in the schools. I would like to see our ministers teaching scriptures to the children in the Druid Hill schools."

"As you know, I'm sure, that wouldn't be permissible under the First Amendment of the Constitution."

"Don't you think the law is unjust, Mrs. Wickman? It was made by men, after all."

"No, I really can't agree with you. Our obligations are to live by laws that have been duly approved and to seek to change those we feel are unjust."

"You know, Mrs. Wickman, God dealt with the evil in me by giving me the power to discern evil in others."

"I don't see much evil, Mrs. Beals, though I find a lot of ignorance and fear."

"There's evil everywhere. I visited one school, and there were student drawings on the walls with witches and monsters and demonic symbols. I walked into the cafeteria in a junior high school, and a black child looked at me. His eyes rolled back and he growled and cursed. That's Satan, Mrs. Wickman. Satan puts thoughts in children's minds."

Meredith couldn't say what she was thinking. Instead, she replied calmly, "I'm glad you're spending some time visiting our schools. I think you'll find we have good teachers here who work hard with our children."

"That makes little difference unless they are working with the children on the right things. Thank you for your time. I just wanted you to know something about my concerns."

"I certainly understand your concerns better now that we have talked. You know, it's not my place to give advice to a new board member, but

I've worked in this district a long time. The long-standing practice of our school board has been for board members to share their individual concerns with the superintendent and fellow board members. If others on the board share those concerns, an appropriate course of action can be determined by the board acting as a collective."

"I appreciate your advice, Mrs. Wickman. I'm sure we'll have a chance to talk again soon."

Mrs. Beals gathered up her purse and her note pad, rose from her chair, and quietly left the room. She certainly didn't look like a woman who would find her cause in rooting out evil. Meredith shuddered as she picked up the telephone to call the superintendent and report on her visitor.

CASE 6.5: SEX SCANDAL IN PONCA HILLS

Allison Macon, director of public relations for Ponca Hills Public School District, made it her custom to get up early in the morning to drink her limit of two cups of freshly ground coffee and read the morning newspapers before she went to the office. She subscribed to three at home: the county weekly, the small daily morning paper published in Ponca Hills itself, and the major state journal published in the state's largest city, about 60 miles from Ponca Hills.

As she unfolded the state journal, she was appalled by the headlines: "Parents: Teachers Led Schoolgirls into Sex Ring." She didn't have to read the lead paragraph to know that the school district in question was Ponca Hills. She had spent most of Monday either talking on the phone to a reporter from the paper or trying to avoid talking to the reporter. She scanned the article to see what the reporter had selected to include:

" . . . four Ponca Hills teachers,"

" . . . at least 25 girls have been involved,"

" . . . seven-year period,"

" . . . county attorney believes some teachers were probably involved in misconduct but no charges will be filed,"

" . . . graduate said sexual relations were forced on her by a teacher,"

" . . . had sex in a car with a teacher,"

" . . . a lot of messing around,"

" . . . they would talk very dirty,"

" . . . claimed sexual involvement with teachers but did not want to press charges,"

" . . . girls were over the age of consent at the time the incidents happened,"

" . . . parents aren't satisfied, even if no laws were broken,"

" ...three Ponca Hills coaches and teachers resigned within days after allegations were made,"

" ...coach said the allegations were ridiculous,"

" ...we felt the evidence proved that these teachers were grooming girls at a relatively young age for future conquests."

She noted that some, though not all, of the information that she and the superintendent had given the reporter appeared in the story: the teachers were no longer with the school district, no charges had been filed, and there was no evidence that the law had been broken. Yet the major newspaper in the state had taken the story—one she believed was a vicious personal vendetta mounted by a few parents against the school district—and turned it into a lurid sex scandal.

The parents had taken their evidence about a sex scandal to district administrators, to the school board, and to the county attorney, none of whom had taken any action. Now the parents had chosen to work through the news media, and the newspaper had become a willing accomplice with a front-page story about accusations that had never been proven against former teachers by former students who refused to press charges.

Allison knew that she would be called to meet with the superintendent as soon as she arrived in the office. She wasn't sure what advice she could give. What could the Ponca Hills administrators, teachers, and school board members do to assure parents who may believe that other teachers have been involved who still work in the district's schools? Should the school board or district administrators make a formal response to the newspaper story? If so, what should it be and how could it ever diminish the impact of a front-page headline about a sex scandal in the public schools?

CASE 6.6: TRAGEDY AT BOARDWALK HIGH SCHOOL

"All I know is that you have to do something, Joe," Frances Smith concluded. "People are terribly concerned. They won't be satisfied if you, as school board president, simply repeat what the experts have been saying. They want action, and I can guarantee you that you can forget about being reelected unless you give them some."

Joe McLaughlin trusted Frances. In their several years on the school board together, she had consistently been the board member most in tune with the sentiments of the community. They had just spent two hours reviewing the recent tragedies at Boardwalk High School and discussing what the school board might do.

It had started two weeks before. Jeff King, a senior wrestler, a healthy, vigorous kid, had died of a staph infection. It seemed outrageous. Jeff was in top physical condition. He was expected to take the state championship in his weight class. Before the wrestle-offs, he had developed a boil on his right arm. Though he put off having it treated because he didn't want to jeopardize his chances in the state tournament, he finally saw a doctor. An operation to locate the source of the infection did not help. He died about a week after he was hospitalized.

If that weren't enough, another Boardwalk student, Lisa Foster, a tenth grader, as much an all-American girl as Jeff King had been an all-American boy, had just died of staphylococcal pneumonia.

The school board and district administrators had been searching for answers. Soon after Jeff died, when school officials first learned that Lisa was seriously ill, school administrators had contacted the county health authorities. Every bit of evidence the health authorities had provided indicated that the two illnesses were coincidence, that nothing in the school building could have caused the infections.

In fact, at the previous Monday night's meeting the school board had heard lengthy testimony from a variety of experts. An epidemiologist with the county health department, Dr. Townsend, testified that reports that dozens of students were being treated for boils resulting from staph infections were simply erroneous. His department was aware of only one other student who was being treated for a boil that might be connected with staph. Five wrestlers who might have had contact with Jeff King had been tested as a precautionary measure, but all were found to be healthy. Dr. Townsend also reported that the school had been inspected the week before and that no health problems were found. He had concluded, "I see no advantage in closing the school."

Experts from the Centers for Disease Control in Atlanta had also been present at the meeting. Most of what they said was general information about staph infections: 40 percent or more of the general population normally carry some staph organisms in their nose or on their hair or skin. Staph organisms normally do no serious harm. Moreover, it would be impossible to clean or disinfect an area such as a high school in order to eliminate staph organisms. Even if it were possible, the organisms would be reintroduced as soon as people entered the building.

Finally, a researcher from the local university reported that results of his tests had confirmed that the two cases of staph among Boardwalk students were caused by totally different strains. The researcher was involved in a study of antibiotic resistance exhibited by some staph strains. He had equipment that could type the staphylococcal organisms by identifying the viruses associated with each. The researcher had concluded with a comment that seemed ironic in retrospect: "This should be good news for concerned parents," he said, "if they will just believe us. There seems to be a lot of emotion in this community right now."

Right after the researcher's presentation, in fact, board member George Jackson had introduced a motion to close the school. His remarks brought applause from many members of the audience, most of whom had only listened politely to the reports from the experts. George's motion had died for lack of a second, but the board did approve a plan suggested by Bob Donaldson, director of buildings and grounds. The plan was little more than a stepped-up program of hygiene: use of a stronger disinfectant, inspection of lockers for cleanliness, briefing of students on hygiene, and the opening of a temporary clinic at the school.

Apparently, the board's action had little effect. About 90 students had been absent from Boardwalk High on the day of the board meeting, about average for the winter months; on the day after the meeting, absences rose to 150, and the next day 230 students were absent. Several parents who had called the school said they intended to keep their children out of school, possibly throughout the week. The next day Lisa died.

Both Joe and Frances were convinced that media coverage had a great deal to do with escalating community concern. While the newspapers had generally carried factual, though extensive, coverage of the events, television stories had been nearly inflammatory. Reporters for two local television stations had interviewed several students about their fears. In fact, Joe had just learned that Boardwalk High's principal, Margaret Langley, had just denied a request from another station to broadcast Lisa's funeral, which would be held in the gymnasium on Saturday.

Superintendent Carrigan would have been particularly helpful in dealing with the media, Joe thought. The assistant superintendents were competent administrators in technical matters, but they tended to repeat the facts as they understood them in interviews with the press. Carrigan would have been more sensitive to public concerns and emotions, but he had been on vacation through much of this. Carrigan had returned home when it became apparent that Lisa was seriously ill, but by then public concern and emotion were already fairly extreme.

Joe still didn't know what to do. Frances had suggested a school board meeting to hear public testimony. They had discussed scheduling it for Sunday afternoon, the day after Lisa's funeral. Joe's concern was that something had to happen as a result of the meeting. The board could not simply hear testimony and agree to do nothing. Though the assistant superintendents and the principal had been telling reporters all week that school would be in session the next week, Joe wasn't so sure. He wanted some information from Bob Donaldson about what a professional cleaning company could do at Boardwalk High School.

Case 6.6: Part II

Joe spent the next two days arranging for the special board meeting and arguing with Bob Donaldson and the other assistant superintendents. All the central office administrators, including the superintendent, believed that time would take care of the problem. Students would start coming back to school; the whole thing would blow over. Donaldson insisted that it would be a waste of tax money to hire a professional cleaning company to fumigate the school. Every company they had contacted had told them that nothing the company could do would kill staph organisms. Medical experts had testified that there was no justification for cleaning the school. Donaldson and the others could not conceive of spending $25,000 for nothing.

Joe finally became adamant. "The board may decide not to hire a professional cleaning company," he told Donaldson and Superintendent Carrigan, "but if they do decide to hire one, I want the contract ready to be signed when the meeting is over, and the company ready to begin the work Sunday night."

Joe spent some time orchestrating Sunday's meeting. Though he was convinced that the medical experts were right, he was equally convinced that the public would not be satisfied until some dramatic action were taken. He was fairly sure that Frances Smith and George Jackson would vote with him on temporarily closing the school and hiring a cleaning company. Mary Anderson and Carter Lewis would as certainly vote against it. He wasn't sure about Sonia Wright, the fourth vote needed for the majority. He had talked the matter over with Frances and arranged for her to introduce a modified resolution in the event that the first vote failed. Sonia had been known to change her mind on heated issues.

He also attended Lisa's funeral. Margaret had been successful in keeping the television cameras out of the high school gymnasium. She couldn't, however, keep them from filming the burial service at the cemetery. That was what the local stations ran on the evening news—that and interviews with students who said they were afraid to go to school.

The meeting Sunday afternoon was orderly. About 273 people showed up. Some were standing in the back and in the hall. The board heard statements from about 30 to 35 people. One person read material from a medical encyclopedia. Several shared personal experiences about medical treatment. Several physicians from the county medical society testified, but people in the audience seemed to discount their testimony as having been solicited by the school district to reassure the public. Only three or four community members stated that they agreed with the expert testimony. Carter Lewis pointed out that 273 people represented only 10 percent of a school district of nearly 25,000. In fact, Carter said he was surprised the crowd wasn't larger.

After the testimony, George Jackson moved that the school be closed for three days and "the best cleaning and sterilizing company we can get," as he put it in his motion, be hired to clean the building. The vote on the motion was 3–3, which meant that the motion failed but that additional motions could be considered.

Then Frances introduced a second motion that essentially repeated the first, with a few technical differences: school would be closed "to assure parents that the building is as clean and safe as it can be and provide some time for students recovering from their grief." The motion passed four votes to two.

Contracts with the two cleaning companies that would do the work were ready for signing. The contracts called for "fumigation and germicidal application" and said that the companies accepted no responsibility for killing staph bacteria. One of the companies began cleaning the building at midnight on Sunday. Television cameras roamed the halls, this time with Margaret Langley's blessing. The evening news carried a story about how many rooms had been cleaned so far.

Classes did not meet at the high school for the two days it took the cleaning company to complete the work. When classes resumed on Wednesday, attendance at Boardwalk High School was above normal.

The cleaning ended the controversy. As Joe later observed on several occasions, no one ever found fault with him for calling the special board meeting or with the board for spending the $25,000 to clean the building. He was reelected to the board. But the irony of it always bothered him. The board's vote was against the recommendations of the administration, against the testimony of experts, against his own assessment of what was required. It was a way of accommodating political outcry, and it was absolutely the right thing to do.

CASE 6.7: DEALING WITH THE PTA PRESIDENT

"People had warned me that she was crazy," continued Hal Burberry, principal of Pine Wood Elementary School. "I probably should have called sooner for advice, but I really didn't think she was *that* crazy and I thought I could handle things myself."

"How did this woman become president of the Parent Teachers Association?" asked Margaret Cochran, Hal's mentor principal during his first year at Pine Wood. "You probably talked about this before, but I've forgotten."

"Last year when Mrs. Williams announced her retirement as principal, it happened that no one wanted to take on the presidency of the

PTA. So Madge Peart became president by default. Everyone was uneasy when that happened because it was widely known that Mrs. Peart has had serious emotional problems. When I arrived, one of the first things I learned was that her children, who are fifth and sixth graders at Pine Wood, had frequently had problems with teachers. One of the senior teachers told me that Mrs. Williams dealt with the Peart children differently because the mother was so difficult. Evidently the special treatment the Peart children had received caused some problems with teacher morale. I was determined to treat these children the same as any other children in the school.''

"What did the band incident have to do with this?'' Margaret Cochran asked.

"Things were going along pretty well until the middle of November. There had been several incidents involving her boys, but we followed normal discipline procedures without repercussions. Then the boys started causing problems for Archer Daniels, the band director. He was trying to rehearse for the annual holiday band concert, and Mrs. Peart's boys began a series of disruptive tactics that nearly finished Archer. In all fairness to Archer, he suffered their pranks with great patience longer than I would have. The pressure for the concert finally made him decide that either the boys had to be removed from band or there could be no concert. So he came to me and asked permission to withdraw the two boys from band. I told him that it was his decision and that, based upon what I knew about the problems, I would certainly back him if that's what he decided was best.''

"Is that when Mrs. Peart went to the superintendent?''

"Well, she came to me first. I told her that we had exhausted the alternatives with the boys, that they would be out of band at least until the beginning of the second semester. I told her it was time that her boys began assuming responsibility for their own actions. I think that's when she decided to involve the superintendent. Parents and teachers had warned me that she would do this, but I had decided to stick by my decision. One person was not going to change my reputation for dealing fairly with kids.''

"Then what happened?''

"The next thing I knew I had a call to show up at central office and meet with the superintendent. So I went. You wouldn't believe the number of ridiculous things that she had told him, and evidently he had believed most of them. Even after I explained in great detail the sequence of events leading up to our decision to pull the children out of band, the superintendent's response conveyed the impression that he somehow blamed me for what had happened. I left his office feeling very angry and frustrated. I felt I had been judged unfairly. Somehow, several members of the PTA executive board learned that Mrs. Peart had gone to the superintendent about me. A group of them banded together and went to see the super-intendent."

"Did you have anything to do with that?"

"I didn't encourage them. They did call me first, and I explained my side of the story without criticizing the superintendent. They didn't ask me for permission to meet with the superintendent, and I didn't discourage them from going."

"How did the superintendent react to the PTA delegation?"

"Well, he told them that he had never believed the mother. For some reason, the board members weren't sure they believed him. They drafted a letter of support for me that was approved at an executive board meeting and sent to the superintendent."

"It's nice to have the support of the school community, isn't it?"

"It sure is. And that wasn't the end of it. The PTA executive board threatened to impeach Mrs. Peart. I, of course, would have nothing to do with that. They ended up scolding her at a board meeting, and they told her to do nothing in the name of the PTA without official board approval. And ever since then, Mrs. Peart has stayed out of my way."

"Now that it's over, do you think you handled the problems with her well?"

"Well, I don't think I did anything unethical or unprofessional. And I certainly applied our policies fairly. But in retrospect, I probably should not have been as aggressive in dealing with her. I probably should have counseled her more and humored her more. I don't think that confronta-tion is the most satisfactory way to deal with someone who has serious mental problems. In fact, I probably could have stopped her from going to the superintendent. On the other hand, my willingness to take Mrs. Peart on and back a teacher was good for the morale of my teachers."

"Well," Margaret said, "it sounds to me as though you've thought this through. It never seems to help one's professional reputation when a parent complains to the superintendent, even if the parent is in the wrong."

CASE 6.8: MRS. COLLINS SPEAKS BEFORE THE BOARD

"Welcome back, Mrs. Collins. What do you have for the school board's consideration this month?" asked Stephen Hoover, school board president.

Stephanie Collins distributed some papers to the members of the board and then walked to the podium. "The issue of concern to me is still my daughter Pamela. I haven't received a response from the board since the last time I spoke to you. As you will recall, my six-year-old daughter has cerebral palsy, and we have been told that the school district cannot provide her with speech and physical therapy because the services being provided are appropriate given Pam's abilities. I don't agree. What the classroom teacher is doing I could easily do at home. Pam needs more help than that. She needs speech and communication skills. She needs physical therapy to help her develop muscle tone. She isn't getting any of that from the teacher now."

Hoover turned to Jeanette Winston, superintendent of schools. "Superintendent, what information can you give us about Mrs. Collins's concerns?"

Superintendent Winston replied, "The district administrator who has responsibility in this area is Betty Bowers, our director of special services. I'd like to ask her to come forward."

Dr. Bowers joined Mrs. Collins at the podium. Hoover repeated the question for her. "What information can you give us about Mrs. Collins's concerns?"

"Let me say as background that Pamela Collins is at an important decision point. Up until the time she turned six, she was receiving services through the Easter Seals Early Intervention program and the State Department of Rehabilitative Services. Now that she is six, the responsibility for the provision of services rests with the school district. Since the last board meeting, we have conducted complete evaluations for speech services, occupational therapy, and physical therapy. In June we administered psychological tests. Our guidelines say that these tests have a six-month validity period. Because the six-month period is about to expire, we're willing to review the data and reevaluate if that seems warranted. Mrs. Collins has asked for reevaluation on several occasions, but our guidelines on reevaluation don't permit retesting within the validity period."

Mrs. Collins interrupted. "If you give Pamela the same kind of tests that you gave her the first time, she'll fail again."

Dr. Bowers responded, "We use the tests that the state approves. Without test results that indicate a need for therapy, the school district's position has been that the child does not meet the criteria for the additional services that Mrs. Collins has requested. We must follow state guidelines on the provision of services, and Pamela simply doesn't qualify," she concluded. "If you have any questions, I'd be glad to respond."

Mrs. Collins stepped back to the microphone. "Pam's classroom teacher has implied that her inability to communicate is due to her lack of intelligence. My daughter has a form of intelligence that is going to put her into society. My husband and I see her trying to communicate. We were dropped by Easter Seals. We were dropped by the state. Insurance companies are taking the same position. Easter Seals taught us how to protect the rights of our children. If necessary, I will ask other parents with special children to join me and we will fill this board room and show you that we can stick together to get the services our children need. If I don't insist on help for Pamela, the system will take until the end of the school year to respond, and my daughter will be the one that loses."

"Dr. Bowers, is she going to get some help?" board president Hoover asked the director of special services.

"We have a meeting scheduled for this coming Thursday so that Mrs. Collins can meet with the supervisor for psychological services, and we will discuss then the state protocols we have to follow," Dr. Bowers replied. "At present, as I said, Pamela doesn't qualify for the services that her parents have requested. State protocols say that we cannot provide services when there is no difference between the child's mental age and developmental functioning. We have also evaluated the need for occupational and physical therapy, again based on state guidelines. That's what we're going to discuss on Thursday.

"We've done everything we can," said Superintendent Winston.

Hoover turned to the superintendent. "So we will get a report at our next meeting regarding this matter?"

"Can each of us get a written summary of your meeting with Mrs. Collins?" asked Madeline Willis, a long-term member of the board.

"I'd like a copy, too," said Mrs. Collins.

Dr. Bowers smiled and said, "We'd be happy to provide a written summary for board members, and we'll send one to you, too, Mrs. Collins. If there are no further questions, thank you." Dr. Bowers returned to her seat in the meeting room.

Mrs. Collins remained at the podium. "When I was in the sixth grade, I chose to do a book report on the life of Helen Keller. Her teacher, Annie Sullivan, didn't give up on Helen Keller, and we're not going to give up on our daughter either. I need your help on this crucial matter."

CASE 6.9: THE SCHOOL BOARD ELECTION

Superintendent of Schools Joseph Farrell knew when he agreed to appear on the noon talk show for WKTZ-TV that the upcoming school board elections would be a main topic of discussion. The host of the show, Mavis Bergman, lost no time in getting to the subject. "Superintendent Farrell, you have traditionally played your political cards close to the vest during prior school board election campaigns. But that was before you became a frequent target of criticism by four of your seven board members, a group you have referred to as the 'negative majority.' Now that your two main critics are seeking reelection, you have shown open support for their challengers. Why the change?"

"Well, Mavis, naturally a superintendent supports a candidate who shares the same philosophy, and I am philosophically in tune with Julia Morgan, who, as you know, is running against board president Jack Phillips, and Martin Daniels, who is running against Bobbie Jackson in the Fourth District."

"While getting ready for this interview, Superintendent Farrell, I called Jack Phillips . . . ."

"Sought out an unbiased source, didn't you?"

"Just looking for a variety of perspectives, Superintendent. Phillips said that the fact that you are an appointed superintendent should have a bearing on your involvement with politics. Let me quote him directly: 'When an appointed superintendent gets involved in the public process of political campaigning, that seems to be improper. It violates the basic premise of an appointed superintendency.' How would you respond to Mr. Phillips?"

"Jack Phillips has a right to his own opinion, but I also have a right to mine. Jack and I have an obvious difference of opinion. I don't run from a fight. It's like racquetball or anything else; I don't like to lose."

"Is it appropriate for you, an appointed superintendent, to take an active role in fund-raising for a candidate who is running against an incumbent board member? I also understand that the fund-raising started during the Fourth of July weekend at a party at your home."

"I don't like the inferences of impropriety in what you're saying, Mavis. If you're talking about Julia Morgan's campaign, the party you're referring to was a Fourth of July party, not a campaign party. If it had been, however, that would have been my privilege. Some of the guests at this party work for the school system, so naturally the conversation included issues about the campaign. It's no secret—I don't support Jack Phillips."

"Our viewers might be interested in why you oppose Jack's re-election."

"Let me talk about why I support Mrs. Morgan, instead. She has children in the public schools. None of the current board members has children in the schools, and I think we need that parental touch, from whoever it might be. Mrs. Morgan has long been a strong advocate of education in this community. She would be an excellent member of the board."

"Then your support of her has nothing to do with the fact that you once fired Jack Phillips, and he has threatened to do the same to you?"

"That has nothing to do with it. As I said before, the real issue in this campaign is the progress of the school system. There are two philosophies represented in the campaign, mine and his. It's obvious that the negative majority want to see a different direction. They must, or they wouldn't want a different superintendent."

"It is true, Superintendent, that Phillips has twice called for your dismissal, and both he and Bobbie Jackson have pledged to vote against renewing your contract."

"I'm not worried about unemployment. I've received numerous offers to run school systems in other states. I could have left long ago if I had wanted to. But as I said before, I don't run from a fight."

"Thank you, Superintendent. I'm sure there's more to be said and more that *will* be said before the election next month, but we're out of time today. My guest today has been Dr. Joseph Farrell, superintendent of schools. We have been discussing the issue of the superintendent's involvement in the election campaigns of candidates for the board of education. We will continue to explore this issue tomorrow when my guest will be Jack Phillips. Join us then."

CASE 6.10: OUR KIDS HAVE BEEN MOVED ENOUGH

Superintendent of Schools Jennifer Bradley was amazed at how the brouhaha had arisen so quickly. The Brookside School District had developed a rational plan for changing the attendance boundaries of four elementary schools. A planning committee, under the direction of Desmond Bennett, the assistant superintendent in charge of community relations, had come up with a plan to relieve overcrowding at Park Elementary. A modest change affecting less than 50 students would balance Park's enrollment with that of three other schools and solve the overcrowding without affecting the racial balance of schools in the district. Brookside District enrolled 21.5 percent minority students, but the state department of education guidelines permitted a 20 percent leeway in minority enrollment at any one school.

The planning committee's proposal had been presented at a school board meeting a week earlier. Few citizens had attended. Those parents who spoke in opposition to the plan were opposed because children who attended schools that were not overcrowded would be moved. In what Jennifer Bradley saw as a classic case of overreaction, the school board had voted against the planning committee's recommendations and given preliminary approval to a proposal initiated by Fritz Benson, the board president, to pair Park school with Fieldhouse, the elementary school closest to it that had available space.

Jennifer had tried to speak strongly against Benson's plan. She warned the board that the pairing arrangement would be a "flagrant violation of state desegregation guidelines." She noted that under Benson's plan minority enrollment at Park would decrease from 57 percent to 52 percent, but Park would still be out of compliance. At the same time, minority enrollment at Fieldhouse would increase from 40 to about 50 percent, putting it out of compliance also. In spite of her arguments, the board voted 4 to 3 for tentative approval. Joe Smith, a prominent black minister in Brookside, was among those voting against the proposal.

Smith worked hard during the week before the special meeting of the board called to reconsider Benson's pairing proposal. He made a few phone calls, talked to a few leaders in the black community, and got people mobilized. At the same time, Jennifer called the Department of Education to check on the legality of the board proposal. John Dean, a State Department of Education staff member, agreed to speak with the board at the special meeting.

The night of the special meeting, the atmosphere was completely different from that of the week before. All the seats were filled, and many in the audience were members of the minority community, including representatives of the local chapter of the NAACP. John Dean testified that the board proposal would not be looked upon favorably by the state. He said that a local board that "knowingly creates" a situation in which a school is out of compliance with state guidelines might suffer different consequences than a board that approves a reorganization action in a "good faith effort" to reduce the number of schools out of compliance. The state, he reminded the board members, has the power to withhold the district's funding or to take over the operation of the district.

Black parents speaking from the audience argued that black children would once again be victims under the board's proposal. One parent argued, "The pairing will put our children on the move again. Over the years our children have had to move, adjust, adjust, and move. Enough is enough. We want you to do what is morally right and vote down the pairing and change the boundaries."

In the end the board had voted against the pairing proposal 7 to 1 and granted preliminary approval to the proposed boundary change. Drew Phillips, one of the board members who changed his vote, said that the pairing plan had been a "trial balloon" and that he would not have supported the plan had "black parents in this area been present and voiced their concerns at last week's meeting."

After the meeting, Jennifer listened as Fritz Benson was interviewed by a local television station. Benson said that although he was not entirely happy with the board's decision to reverse itself, he felt that "the process has been affirmed." He concluded, "We don't make these decisions on one-evening stands."

Jennifer smiled. She really wasn't so sure.

CASE 6.11: BIDDING ON MOLE CRICKET CONTROL

As Walt Gooding returned to his office as school business manager for the Elmcrest Metropolitan School District, his secretary, Tootie Bailey, handed him a message from Bill Pinkney, commercial sales representative for A Touch of Grass. Pickney's company, a local lawn maintenance business, had submitted a bid on the contract to provide mole cricket control for the district. He had phoned early in the morning and requested that Walt return his call. Walt was pretty sure he knew what Pinkney wanted. The school board had met the night before and had awarded a contract for care of the district's athletic fields to a competing firm, even though A Touch of Grass had submitted the low bid.

He dialed Pinkney's number and asked for his extension. "Good afternoon, Mr. Pinkney. How can I help you?"

"I'd like to ask you some questions about the contract on the athletic fields, especially about the provision for mole cricket control. First, I was at the board meeting last night and was just amazed when the contract was awarded to a competitor whose bid was 45 percent higher than ours."

"Well, Mr. Pinkney, the board's obligation is to award the bid to the lowest *qualified* bidder. That's what the board did in this instance."

"I'd like to know what disqualified our bid?"

"As you know, we've had severe damage to the school district athletic fields caused by mole crickets. We asked for a treatment compound that includes a five percent malathion solution. Your bid did not meet this specification."

"Remember what I pointed out to you a couple of weeks ago, Mr. Gooding. The product you asked for in the bid specifications hasn't been made in the United States for seven years and hasn't been made abroad for 18 months. We included what we felt was a qualified substitute. I told you that we would stand by our prices and guarantee our product and service and that we would buy the specified product if you could find anybody to produce it. That was the best we could do, given the circumstances."

"The company that submitted the successful bid indicated it could meet the specifications for malathion."

"First of all, are the school board members aware that the specimen label included in the winning bid was made on the company's personal computer? All the other bids you received were for products that are registered with the Environmental Protection Agency. The bid you accepted has no EPA registration on it. Anybody can mix up chemicals to make a product, but there is no guarantee of quality. You're going to apply this stuff to football and baseball fields. As a former football and baseball player, I have some concerns about that. The board really needs to consider the possibility of a liability suit, because the product in the winning bid is not EPA registered."

"Mr. Pinkney, let me assure you that we reviewed the bids thoroughly and checked the product specifications again with both our local maintenance people and the county extension agent. They assured us that the approved bid provides an acceptable means of treatment for mole crickets."

"I think that the board should reconsider its decision and that this contract should be rebid. When you send something out for bids, your specifications should not include a product that is not even produced commercially. What you have here is a single-source bid. You had only one company out of 17 that bid it correctly. That in itself should have told you something. I'm surprised board members didn't ask questions about this and ask you to reconsider."

"Well, the fact is they didn't, Mr. Pinkney."

"I just want to tell you once more that we will stand by our prices and guarantee our service. I plan to appear before the board at the next meeting and bring these things to their attention. I think the taxpayers would like to know how irresponsibly this has been handled."

CASE 6.12: THE TALENT SHOW

Garfield Junior High School was a sprawling old building located in the central part of the city. The school had been enlarged several times through additions, and the corridors seemed to be blocks long. Garfield enrolled 1,100 students in grades seven, eight, and nine, but ninth graders were to be moved to the high schools the next year because of declining high school enrollments. Data about the student body composition of junior high schools in the Middle City School District are summarized in the table next page. While the racial and ethnic composition of Garfield's student body was not unusual for the school district, minority groups were concentrated in the seventh and eighth grades. Because of the district's busing plan, ninth graders tended to live primarily in the white, middle-class neighborhoods surrounding the school rather than in the black and Hispanic areas west and south of the school.

John Marks, principal of Garfield, had come up through the ranks in the Middle City Schools as a teacher, assistant principal, and principal. He had developed a reputation as a no-nonsense disciplinarian who adopted a hard-and-fast rule about rules: "We have rules which, when broken, specify a punishment. They apply to everyone without exception. End of discussion." Teachers at Garfield were delighted when Marks was appointed as principal there. After years of working under a principal who could not make decisions, most teachers preferred John's uncompromising approach to student discipline. While no teacher ever accused John of racial or ethnic prejudice, some teachers thought he lacked sensitivity and

**RACIAL COMPOSITION OF JUNIOR HIGH SCHOOLS,
MIDDLE CITY PUBLIC SCHOOLS**

	American Indian or Alaskan		Asian		Hispanic		Black		White	
	No.	%	No.	%	No.	%	No.	%	No.	%
Adams	37	2.4	15	1.0	70	4.6	281	18.6	1108	73.4
Coolidge	13	1.2	8	0.7	9	0.8	212	19.8	829	77.5
Eisenhower	25	1.5	8	0.5	26	1.6	740	44.9	850	51.5
Garfield	4	0.4	17	1.5	16	1.4	346	31.1	730	65.6
Hamilton	0	0.0	2	0.5	50	13.2	51	13.5	275	72.8
Jefferson	8	0.6	6	0.5	4	0.3	394	31.6	834	67.0
Kennedy	16	1.3	44	3.5	26	2.1	362	29.1	795	64.0
Lincoln	6	0.5	4	0.4	11	1.0	429	38.4	666	59.7
Madison	26	2.6	20	2.0	44	4.3	228	22.6	690	68.5
Wilson	1	0.1	3	0.4	1	0.1	178	22.8	598	76.6
Totals	**136**	**1.2**	**127**	**1.1**	**257**	**2.3**	**3,221**	**29.0**	**7,375**	**66.4**

saw him as too rigid, too quick to apply the rules. Central office administrators appeared to support his administrative approach. Although he had been the target of a few complaints by community minority groups, he had been recommended for promotion to a high school principalship several years before and was frequently mentioned as a likely candidate to replace a current high school principal who was about to retire. John was not a man of vision, but he was predictable and dependable and he carried authority with parents and students.

John was proud of the school and Garfield students. He had gone out of his way to make the ninth graders' last year at Garfield special. Students were urged to do especially well because each event would be the last: the last football season, the last band concert, the last school play. The last talent show, in the spring, was given similar attention.

The talent show was always a big event, but this year Garfield pride was at stake. Each group that was to perform was urged to match or outdo the performances of previous years. While faculty sponsors frequently had to impress on the student authors the fact that skits must be previewed by the principal, those who had been around for a while had noted that the Garfield performances were not immune from the influences of popular television shows and had become more risqué and at times nearly offensive. A skit a couple of years before that contained innuendoes about homosexuals was frequently used as an example of how times had changed.

John didn't anticipate any problems with the talent show this year. He knew there were a number of teachers he could count on, such as Ted Jamison, the drama teacher who had been directing the talent show for several years. Others, such as Fred Knowles, were more likely to do something a bit squirrely. The International Club he sponsored included some of the brightest, cleverest kids in the school. Fred was distrusted by faculty, and John saw him as always having to be right, to have the last word, and to show up everyone else.

John was particularly busy the week of the talent show. Every administrative office in the district seemed to have something that needed to be done immediately. When he saw Ted Jamison in the hall, Ted assured him that dress rehearsals had gone well. John had stopped in several times and seen parts of various skits, but the afternoon performance for students was the first time John saw all 30 acts. The performance by the school band was good, but predictably too long. The gymnastics group once again demonstrated that liability insurance was a continuing necessity. And the International Club presented a near-professional parody of a popular television show titled "Wheel of Misfortune," an elaborate game show in which contestants from various ethnic groups competed for prizes such as heat for a month in the Booker T. Washington housing project in the southwest part of the city, dinner for twelve and coupons for five loads of laundry at the Duds and Suds Diner and Laundry, a one-way ticket to Puerto Rico, and a '72 pink Cadillac complete with fuzzy dice and a nodding dog in the back window.

Following the student matinee, Annie Immervahr, a veteran English teacher who had just been chosen by her colleagues as their nominee for teacher of the year, told John she felt the skit by the International Club was in poor taste. She cornered him when he was trying to get out of the building for a meeting with a local business group, and she did not mince words: "Inappropriate, totally inappropriate," was the way she put it. John wasn't so sure. The skit seemed no more offensive to him than several of the television shows his own children thought were hilarious. On his way out of the building, though, he stopped a couple of teachers and asked them how they felt about the International Club's skit. Those he talked to said they had talked to a few students themselves and the kids thought it was funny.

Later that evening, John relaxed and enjoyed the public performance for over 800 parents and community members. He had reason to reconsider his feelings of assurance when the phone calls started to come in the next day complaining that the International Club skit had been offensive and degrading to minority members in the community. The president of the local chapter of the NAACP called and told John that he would not rest until "this affront to our people has been redressed." A prominent leader in the Hispanic community called and argued that this was just one more example of the rampant racism at Garfield Junior High School. This woman was well-known to John as a perennial troublemaker whose daughter recently had made an accidental injury received in a girls' volleyball game appear to be the result of a malicious and racially motivated attack.

By early afternoon, John decided he had better call Dr. Charles Singer, the superintendent of schools, to let him know about the reactions he was getting from the community. Dr. Singer listened without comment, advised John not to get too defensive, and asked to be kept informed if anything else happened. Dr. Singer also suggested that Marks might write a letter of explanation and apology to groups that might have been offended by the skit. Singer then called one of his assistant superintendents and asked her to look into the situation and report back to him. Back at Garfield, John Marks mulled things over. What should he do next?

Case 6.12: Part Two

The next morning, after the buses had been unloaded, John met with his assistant principals to discuss the situation. The assistant principals suggested that no real damage had been done, that the vituperative phone calls had been made by sensation-seeking kooks, and that the crisis would soon blow over. Although generally reassured, John was still a bit uneasy. His worst fears were realized later in the day when Tony Gonzalez, the director of the Hispanic Cultural Center, and three other men stormed into his office and confronted him. They demanded his resignation, threatened to take matters into their own hands if nothing was done, and left as abruptly as they had come. Thirty minutes later John received an emergency summons to Fred Knowles's classroom, where he found the four men standing outside in the hall. The men said that they merely wanted to talk to Knowles but that he had refused to leave his classroom. John insisted that they were violating school visitation policies and asked them to leave immediately. After muttering a few obscenities, the four left the building.

Walking back to his office, John realized that satisfying Gonzalez was not going to be easy. The two of them went back a long way. In fact, his first recollection was the time Tony had cornered him at a local bar in the west end of town and accused him of making life tough for Hispanic children at Highland High School, where John was assistant principal. Other incidents had occurred from time to time that had perpetuated an adversarial relationship between the two. Was this more evidence of a vendetta? Was Tony out to destroy him? John was sure of one thing: the controversy surrounding the skit was being fueled from outside the school system. He probably ought to write the letter that Dr. Singer suggested.

Case 6.12: Part Three

At the regular meeting of the Board of Education's Instructional Committee the following week, Gonzalez and the NAACP chapter president requested a place on the agenda and proceeded to testify that the International Club skit was an example of racism at its worst. They argued that the faculty and administration at Garfield School were aiding and abetting this travesty. Gonzalez told committee members that he had personally read the script for the skit after a concerned parent called him to say that she was shocked by it. This concerned parent, John later learned, was the mother of one of the authors of the skit and an employee of the newspaper that was continuing to print extensive coverage of the incident. After hearing from the minority spokespersons, the board committee members agreed that an apology written on behalf of the school district was called for, noted that Marks had already authored an apology to minority groups in the community, and hoped that the matter was closed.

The next week the skit at Garfield was discussed at the regular meeting of the full school board. Eight students who had performed in the controversial skit offered apologies and said that they had not intended to insult or demean any group. One student said, "We're very sorry. We did not mean any harm. We never thought of it that way." Representatives from the Hispanic Cultural Center followed the students and restated their complaints. They demanded demotion of John Marks and termination of employment for Fred Knowles. Several parents spoke in defense of Garfield Junior High School and John Marks.

At the end of this part of the meeting, Dr. Singer reported to the board that he would "take appropriate action" in disciplining the teacher and principal but noted that "It is the policy of this school district to keep personnel actions of this nature confidential." He concluded his remarks with words of conciliation: "I apologize for this incident to those groups who have expressed concern and hope that we can all learn from this unfortunate experience."

Fanny McMillan, spokesperson for the NAACP, told a local reporter after the meeting, "These generalities aren't worth a hill of beans. At some point, somebody needs to be made an example of. I think school officials are more interested in protecting their own people than achieving quality education for minority students." Her comments were reported in the morning paper. When a reporter called Marks and asked him for a response, John had no comment.

Responses to the incident continued to come in. The local newspaper continued its coverage in both the morning and evening editions, the Human Relations Committee of the city council passed a resolution condemning the skit at Garfield Junior High, a black state senator introduced a resolution in the state legislature that censured the school, and Dr. Singer published a formal apology on behalf of the school district.

Later that week, when the superintendent of schools chaired a regular meeting of the district's community relations staff, one of John Marks's supporters asked a pointed question during the closing minutes of the meeting. "You say we are all family," he began, "but one of our family has really been hurt recently. What have we done and what are you going to do to help John Marks?" The superintendent's response was guarded. He reviewed the events relating to the skit, said it was all unfortunate, a terrible mistake. When John heard about the meeting, he found no words of comfort in what the superintendent had said. The matter wasn't finished yet. Meanwhile the school district grapevine was broadcasting the message that John didn't have a chance of being promoted to high school principal now.

Case 6.12: Part Four

By the time he received a call from the superintendent's secretary summoning him to a conference with Dr. Singer, John felt that he had been abandoned by his superiors and that he was all alone. No one in central administration had come to his defense. What little encouragement he had received had come from his own staff and a few parents. Teachers at Garfield, and John too, felt that the whole incident had been blown out of proportion, that they were being unfairly portrayed as insensitive and racist. A single unfortunate incident was being used to suggest that this was only the most recent and visible example of rampant institutional racism.

In his meeting with John, Dr. Singer again reviewed the details of the incident. After John was given a chance to speak on his own behalf, Dr. Singer told him that he would not be terminated or demoted. Instead, John's punishment would be to prepare three written statements giving his personal views about minority groups and measures the public schools could take to better serve them, and in addition to give forty hours of community service. John didn't respond. He didn't know what to say. While he had suspected that someone would have to be punished, and that, as chief administrator at the school, he was the obvious target, he was extremely disappointed and hurt. It was little consolation to him that Fred Knowles received the same punishment later that day.

Two days later Knowles filed a grievance against the administration of the school district. The president of the local teachers' union, speaking on Knowles's behalf, claimed that the administration had not followed its own grievance procedures, which required that complaints against faculty must first be submitted in writing to the school principal and then could be appealed to the superintendent and school board. The superintendent responded only that the controversy had come to him full-blown in the morning newspaper and he had no choice but to act outside of the formal grievance process. Later that day John learned from Garfield's union representative that Knowles planned to argue in the hearing that he considered himself free of responsibility since Marks had viewed the skit during the matinee performance and dress rehearsals and had not objected to it at any time.

John wondered, as he walked to his car to go home, if it would ever end. He also knew it was quite possible that he might be the only one to be punished to protect minority rights in the school district. He had put in twenty years of hard work in this district. It wasn't fair!

CHAPTER 7

Managing Culture

The culture or social heritage of any society is always specific; it is the distinctive way of life of a group of people, their complete design for living.

Clyde Kluckhohn

CASE 7.1: THE SQUIRT GUN

Karen couldn't believe what she was seeing! Here she was, in one of her first observations as science supervisor for the Jackson Consolidated School District, and Jeff Fredrickson, a high school science teacher, had just squirted a student with a squirt gun in the middle of a chemistry class. Karen knew that the student hadn't been paying attention. Jeff had certainly taken care of that problem. She also knew that the information that Jeff had been presenting about safety in the chemistry lab was really important. Still, Jackson Public Schools had a strict and controversial district policy on weapons in school. If teachers used guns as toys in class, that policy would be even more difficult to enforce. There were any number of other ways to get a student's attention, and she was sure that Jeff had done absolutely the wrong thing. She was so upset, in fact, that when she later ran into Principal Anderson in the hall, she told him what had happened.

The next day, when Karen was back at the high school for more observations, she saw Jeff standing outside his classroom door. She walked over and said, "I would like to talk to you sometime...." Before she could finish, Jeff said, "The gun is gone," turned, and walked into his classroom. Dr. Anderson had obviously talked to him first. The squirt gun had been taken care of, but Karen had the feeling that she had lost a much more important battle.

CASE 7.2: RECOGNIZING OUR TEACHERS

Frances Thurber looked over the crowd at the annual Midlands Public Schools Teacher Recognition Breakfast. As always, the ballroom was full for this event. Organizing the breakfast and arranging the program had never been an enjoyable part of her job as assistant superintendent, but that didn't stop her from feeling some pride on the day of the event. Most of the people who were to share the head table with her had already arrived, and several people were still trying to find their places at other tables.

It wasn't easy to get 900 people together for anything at 7:30 in the morning. She was surprised at how many of the guests she didn't know. She knew the central office staff, of course. Businesspeople who had partnerships with local schools had been invited, and she didn't know most of them. She knew the school principals, but each principal could bring a guest representing the school. She assumed that most of the other people she didn't know were members of the parent associations. The head table was completed by the arrival of Justin Kingsley, a local television personality who would serve as master of ceremonies.

Once again the hotel did an acceptable job of serving the meal. While the food was only a bit better than mediocre, the service was quick and efficient, and the servers made sure that each table had access to fresh coffee. While Frances ate, she noticed two teachers from the education association who were seated at a table off to the right. They seemed to be counting people at the tables and getting more and more agitated. Margaret Lankin was one of them. Frances made a mental note to chat with her later. She liked to keep in touch with the association.

After most people had finished their breakfast, Justin Kingsley started the program. He began by asking groups in the audience to stand to be recognized: the mayor and city council members, members of the school board, central office administrators, business partners for the schools, representatives of the parent associations. Then with a few jokes he launched into his introduction of the superintendent, who was to be the speaker. "Oh no," Frances thought, "he omitted the teachers."

The superintendent's remarks were brief and predictable. The board president and the mayor both talked about the importance of education to the economic development of the community. The program ended in time to allow most people to get to work by 9:00 A.M., the time when many of the district's elementary schools began the student day.

On her way out of the ballroom, Frances stopped to greet Margaret Lankin. Margaret was obviously upset. "Frances," she began, "the school district has done it again. You sponsor a breakfast to recognize teachers and there were less than 90 teachers in the audience. That's less than 10 percent, Frances. When are you administrators going to wake up?"

CASE 7.3: THE PARKING LOT

When she agreed to accept the job at Woodrow Wilson Junior High School, Gladys knew that the change would not be easy. While she was an experienced principal, all of her experience had been in elementary schools. She had not even taught at the secondary level. Still, Superintendent Ackers felt Gladys could do the job. Gladys also knew she would be replacing a minority principal who was well-known in the neighborhood. Her predecessor's failure to monitor the work of the faculty and staff was a primary reason for his transfer, though of course she couldn't explain that to anyone.

She had met her office staff the week before. The two assistant principals were experienced though undistinguished administrators, both men. The secretarial staff consisted of two clerk-typists and one receptionist-typist, Mrs. Begley. Mrs. Begley was going to be a problem. Gladys had heard from many of her acquaintances in the school district that Mrs. Begley, who had worked at Wilson for nearly twenty years, ran the school. She knew most of the families in the neighborhood, she gave and withheld information to exert her influence, and she was a notorious gossip. As the first woman principal at Wilson after a long history of relatively weak, but much loved, male administrators, Gladys knew it wouldn't be easy to convince Mrs. Begley that she, not Mrs. Begley, intended to be the chief executive at Woodrow Wilson.

The next week when Gladys officially reported for work, Mrs. Begley was not there. She had taken a week of vacation time. Gladys had not even begun to get settled in her office when the first teacher stopped in to check on her parking space in the west lot. Several others followed, though teachers were not on contract until the next week. Gladys soon learned that parking was an important concern for staff at Wilson. Though the school had two lots for faculty and staff, an east lot and a west lot, faculty preferred the west lot, which was closer to the main office. Competition for space in the west lot sometimes became heated. She also learned that Mrs. Begley had for several years used the most desirable space in the west lot, the one just next to the entrance.

Gladys thought about the situation for a couple of days, assuring faculty as they stopped by that parking spaces would be assigned by the time faculty officially reported for work on Monday. In the meantime, she called an old friend in the Department of Buildings and Grounds and arranged to have a painting crew at the school at the end of the week to mark the spaces in the west and east lots.

When the crew arrived, Gladys met them in the west lot. She asked them to mark the space nearest the entrance, Mrs. Begley's old space, with the word "Principal" and to put "Assistant Principal" in the two spaces next to it. The rest of the spaces were to be numbered.

Later that day, as faculty continued to drift in and out of the building, Gladys noticed several whispered conversations in the halls. As she passed a group of male staff members she thought she could trust, she asked them what was going on. "Faculty pool," said one of them, "betting on what Mrs. Begley will do when she returns from vacation on Monday. Don't be surprised, Gladys, if she drives into that space as if your car weren't there."

"It'll be there," Gladys replied, "and Mrs. Begley will find it there every workday during the next school year. That you can bet on."

CASE 7.4: THE BUNNY AT JEFFERSON HIGH SCHOOL

Thirty minutes before the pep rally to send the boys' basketball team off to the state tournament was to begin, Assistant Principal Otis Perkins had heard enough through the grapevine to know that something unusual was going to happen. He passed what little he knew on to Principal Joel Glasser, who quickly gathered the administrative team: Marvin Johnson, athletic director; Margaret Gillian, dean of girls; Armand Conley, dean of boys; and himself. Their strategy, they decided, would be to avoid over-reacting; Jefferson had a long-standing tradition of senior pranks, most of which were harmless.

As 1,500 students gathered in the school gymnasium while the pep band played, Otis enjoyed the scene. Johnson would be the master of ceremonies for the program. When he walked up to the microphone at one end of the gymnasium, several students in the crowd booed. Johnson was not a favorite with many of the students. He was authoritarian by nature, rarely gave ground in dealings with students, and had in past months ejected several students from basketball games whom he suspected of drinking before the games.

The rally was being held to salute several school teams that had finished their seasons—the varsity wrestling team, the swim team, and the girls' basketball team—in addition to celebrating the advancement of the boys' basketball team to the state tournament. Students were enthusiastic as each of the teams was called to the front and awards were distributed.

Otis could see that Joel Glasser, who was standing off to his left at the back of the crowd, was proud of the students, both those being honored and those in the audience.

Finally, members of the boys' basketball team were called to the front, each escorted by a member of the pep squad. As Johnson began talking about the importance of all students representing the school well at the state tournament, a young woman stood up in one of the front rows of the bleachers and began to remove her school sweatshirt and jeans. Student attention turned to her as she revealed her costume—an unbuttoned tuxedo jacket, a tight low-cut body suit, fishnet hose with a red garter on her right leg, and high heels. As she hopped down from the bleachers, she placed a set of bunny ears on her head and moved toward the front of the crowd.

She took the microphone from Marvin Johnson, kissed him loudly on the cheek, and began her routine. "Have you had any fun lately, Marvin?" she asked.

Johnson turned red, but gamely said that he'd had some fun.

"Marvin, I want to know whether you are getting enough?"

Johnson shook his head.

"Marvin, I'm here to help you get it on."

While some students cheered and others looked around to see how teachers and administrators were reacting, the young woman continued her banter. "I'd like you to help me out here," she said, as she pulled a pair of lace panties from her pocket.

Johnson took the panties when she handed them to him. "No," she said, "you'll need your hands free. Let me just put them here," she said as she slipped the panties on his head.

Otis could see the beads of sweat on Johnson's face. "Now help me take off this garter, Marvin. To make it a real challenge, you can't use your hands. Maybe you could use your teeth."

Otis looked over at Joel Glasser and located Margaret Gillian at the other side of the gym. Both looked frozen in space, impassive, incredulous.

Johnson leaned over the young woman's leg, then suddenly stood upright and said, "That's it. The joke is over." He took the microphone back as the young woman turned toward the door. He said only enough to dismiss the students and gestured to the director of the pep band to start the music. As students filed from the gymnasium, Joel Glasser headed toward the front of the gym and Otis followed behind.

When Joel reached Marvin, Marvin grabbed his arm and leaned heavily on him. Marvin's school sweater was soaked with sweat, his face was beet red, and he was breathing heavily. "I should have unplugged the microphone," Joel said. He patted Marvin's back and said, "It's okay, Marvin, you kept things from getting too much out of hand."

That wasn't, however, how the story in the newspaper the next morning described it. A local reporter had interviewed both Joel and Bill Logan, the owner and manager of Personal Touch Message Service. Joel was quoted as saying that a small group of students had hired the bunny as a joke to embarrass the athletic director. Logan said, "The kids loved it. The principal wasn't too happy, though." As he described it, a group of kids had wanted to do something dramatic for the athletic director to wish him and the team good luck for the tournament. The students who contacted him had asked for a male stripper, but he had told them that his firm could furnish only bunnies or balloons. The "sexy bunny" routine, he said, costs $50 and includes jokes and improvisations by the woman "gauged to embarrass a man but all in good fun." Finally, Joel was reported as saying, "We are not ignoring the situation."

Later that day, Joel called a meeting of the administrative team. Johnson was absent, because he was escorting the team to the state tournament. Students who had been instrumental in hiring the bunny had been identified through the signature of one of them on the order form. Joel had talked to the student, David Fitzsimmons, early in the day. David had shown no reluctance about naming the students who had gone with him to arrange for the joke and had collected money contributed by more than 60 students. His only explanation was that Johnson had been "giving us a lot of hassle" and they just wanted to put a stop to it. They didn't know any other way to "make Johnson back off," he said.

The purpose of the meeting, Joel said, was to make sure that they all agreed about how the bunny incident would be handled from here on. He had already met with several of the students who had been involved. The students had agreed that there would be no more senior pranks for the rest of the year. Several seemed embarrassed about the publicity this one had received. Joel said he had a meeting scheduled in an hour with David Fitzsimmons's parents. He didn't think that the school should discipline the other students involved.

Armand Conley disagreed: "These kids have no respect. Kids need limits. They'll keep pushing the limits unless lines are drawn for them. Things have become too loose around here. If we do nothing, we're sending the wrong message to kids."

"Armand," Joel said, "I understand your feelings, but we can't punish 50 or 60 students who contributed fifty cents or a dollar to play a joke on Marvin Johnson. How could we ever defend that action with parents?"

Margaret and Otis agreed with Joel. "It happened," Joel said. "It's over. I'm sure it won't happen again."

"What do you think will happen to Marvin?" Margaret asked.

"I don't think anything will," Joel said. "I've had a few phone calls from parents and others calling for his resignation, but the superintendent and members of the board of education weren't among them."

Margaret, who had looked uncomfortable through most of the meeting, finally asked the question that had been on her mind. "Several people have told me that they don't understand how an incident like this could have happened. I'm not sure I understand it either. Joel, what should we have done differently? What should we have done?"

CASE 7.5: THE POLICY ON DELIVERIES TO STUDENTS

"It all started with one or two singing telegrams," concluded Brian Gant, principal of Sherman Senior High School. "Then it began to mushroom. Now, almost daily, there are deliveries of balloons, bouquets, candy, and last week a belly dancer. That's why I say we need a district-wide policy on deliveries to students."

Superintendent Vinnetta Ellis, who was chairing the meeting of the school district administrative team, said, "What do you suggest, Brian?"

"I say we need to put a stop to it," Brian responded. "Students began remembering each other's birthdays and special occasions by calling Hire a Memory, a firm downtown that specializes in what they call 'hand-delivered commemoratives.' This seemingly harmless gesture has grown to unmanageable proportions. Do you know that we now receive between five and ten surprise deliveries a week?"

"Any comments from anyone else?" Vinnetta asked.

Nellie Lombardo, principal of the middle school, said, "I can appreciate how disruptive this has become, and I'm concerned about it beginning in my school. But how can we distinguish between the occasional delivery of balloons and flowers that some of the school clubs use for fund-raisers and the delivery of messages by private firms or the more 'exotic' deliveries that students might order for a joke?"

"That's a sticky question, Nellie," Vinnetta responded.

"What I'd suggest," said Jean Melcher, assistant superintendent for business, "is that we send a notice to this firm that unless they get prior permission from the principal for a delivery, they will be considered as trespassing on school grounds and we will call the police to have them arrested."

"I'm not sure that's legal. Besides, that would set our relationships with the local business community back considerably. What other options do we have?"

Vinnetta thought a moment. "Why don't we put this on the agenda for next week. I'll contact the school attorney and see what the legal parameters are. In the meantime, Brian, why don't you call Hire a Memory and tell them that you'd appreciate it if they suspended deliveries until we develop a policy on this. You might explain what the problems are and ask them if they would be willing to work with us on this."

CASE 7.6: THE CHANGE OF GRADE

Mrs. Violet Rasmussen was waiting for Principal Keith Bonett when he arrived at his office in Ed Gillette Senior High School. Her appearance at his office was not unexpected because he knew that she and her son Mark's English teacher, Sandy Dollar, had come to an impasse in a lengthy and heated telephone conversation the day before.

Sandy had reported the problem to him late in the afternoon and told him that Mrs. Rasmussen intended to bring her concern to Keith immediately. Sandy had outlined the circumstances that had led up to the telephone call. Mark had received a final grade of "F" in English Four. Because he would not receive credit for his final semester of English, he was short of the credits required for graduation.

As Keith ushered Mrs. Rasmussen into his office, he knew that he wanted to avoid involving Sandy in the confrontation if at all possible. She had a very fragile personality and was easily upset by conflict. Sandy had a reputation for being an excellent teacher, but she was not effective in dealing with angry parents. He knew that from previous experience.

"I'm sure you can help me, Mr. Bonett. Mark has never been an outstanding student, but he has never failed any of his courses. Based on his grades this semester, I don't think that he failed this one. There must be some mistake, but I can't seem to get Mrs. Dollar to understand."

"According to Mrs. Dollar, Mark's overall English average simply was not high enough. She could do nothing but give him an 'F' for the term."

"But that's not what she said, Mr. Bonett. Here, take a look at the progress report we received in the middle of the fourth quarter. You can see that the note from Mrs. Dollar at the bottom says that if Mark earned at least a 'C' for the last grading period, he would pass the course and receive credit. When the guidance counselor called yesterday morning to tell me that Mark would not graduate, I couldn't believe it. I asked the counselor why, and he said that Mark had failed English. So I called Mrs. Dollar. I had been checking on Mark's grades for this term, and I knew he was passing. She told me that Mark had passed the fourth quarter but he had a failing average for the term."

"I see."

"It's just not fair. She promised he would pass if he worked hard and got a 'C.' He did that, and she still failed him. But she had put it in writing, Mr. Bonett. Isn't she legally obligated to do what she promised?"

"I've always known Mrs. Dollar to be fair and very precise and thorough in her evaluations of students. I'll have to talk to Mrs. Dollar more about this and get back to you."

"We were having a party for Mark, and we've asked relatives from a hundred miles away. It would be a real problem for our family if Mark cannot graduate with his class."

Keith asked Sandy Dollar to meet with him during her planning period later that morning. He described his meeting with Mrs. Rasmussen and said, "Sandy, are you absolutely certain that you calculated Mark's average for the semester correctly?"

"Yes, I am, Keith. I recomputed it several times. His grade for the third quarter was just so low that the fourth-quarter grade didn't compensate for it, though he came within a few points of passing. I'm sorry about it, but I've always treated kids the same. Either they have enough points to pass the course, or they fail. Mark failed."

"What about what you wrote on Mark's progress report? Mrs. Rasmussen saved that report, you know, with your comment on the bottom that said he would pass the semester if he received at least a 'C' in the final grading period."

"I now regret that I did that. I really thought he had a chance, and I wanted to encourage him to do his best for the rest of the year."

Later that day Keith made the promised contact with Mrs. Rasmussen, knowing that what he had to tell her would not be what she wanted to hear. During his conversation with her, he reported that Mrs. Dollar had demonstrated to him that the final grade was an honest reflection of what Mark had earned in senior English. "I'm sorry that this happened," he said, "but Mark can still graduate by making up the credit in summer school. He can still get his diploma."

"Will you let Mark participate in the ceremony? Graduation has always been a special occasion in our family."

"I'm sorry, it would be unfair to the other graduates who have completed all of their work successfully."

"I'm very sorry you feel that way. You leave me no choice but to involve our attorney in this. I've already spoken with him, and, as an old family friend, he's very willing to represent us. He will be contacting you within the next day or two."

As Keith hung up the telephone, he reminded himself that he had been through lawsuits before, and he tried to avoid them whenever possible. He wanted to look at the alternatives available to him, though he honestly didn't see many. He could go back to Sandy to see if she would be willing to reconsider the grade. There was no other way to certify Mark for graduation, because he lacked both credit and the English requirement. He could contact the school district attorney. He wasn't sure whether a teacher's comments on a progress report constituted a contractual obliga-

tion. Should he be less concerned about appearances and let Mark participate in the graduation ceremony, even though other students were likely to
know that Mark was not graduating? One thing was certain: he was going
to insist that policies about notifying parents about student progress be
revised.

CASE 7.7: TEACHING THE NEW PRINCIPALS

Edgewood Community School District conducts its own managerial
training program for aspiring administrators. The program consists of a
series of seminars designed to familiarize novices with administrative
procedures in the district, with the district's special programs, and with
community resources. The final seminar has traditionally been a presentation by the superintendent of schools. At the concluding session for
the current group of trainees, Superintendent Antonio Guerra rose to
give his remarks.

"Good afternoon. I'm always pleased to have the opportunity to speak to
the men and women from whom we will select our new assistant principals,
administrative interns, and central office support staff.

"I am personally involved in the selection of new administrators. I
consider it my special responsibility to make sure there is a match between
the values of this organization and the values of those we select as leaders.
Therefore, I think it is important for you to know more about what I value
in an administrator and the norms we have tried to establish for leaders in
the Edgewood Community Schools.

"First of all, administrators who are successful in this district have a
strong work ethic. They are willing to work full days and extra hours when
needed. They are willing to go the extra mile.

"Second, they have positive regard for people. They firmly believe
that people want to work and want to be successful. When confronted with
problems or concerns of others, they are extremely good listeners; as
administrators, they see their role as working to unleash the abilities of
others to be successful.

"This leads me to identify a term that I find very distasteful: the term
'arrogance' suggests to me what successful administrators must avoid.
Arrogance negates those characteristics I see as strengths. I don't want
administrators working in this district who believe they are better than
those they serve, who are unable to grow and change, and who express in
their attitudes the notion that 'I'm the administrator; therefore, I'm the
best.'

"Instead, I want administrators who are open to new ideas and have
the skills to develop a culture of high expectations.

"Our managerial training program is intended to do more than indoctrinate you with a specific organizational perspective. We have established this program to model the behaviors we expect you to utilize when you assume administrative responsibility. For example, I am standing here telling you something about my values. I will expect you to do the same with your subordinates. Tell them what you stand for, be willing to expose what you believe. Then, as is inevitable, when you do something that is inconsistent with your own stated values, your subordinates will remind you; they will be willing to point out the contradictions. I expect you to do that for me. I would expect you to be willing to accept it from others.

"An area of concern for many aspiring school administrators is the relationship between their own good judgments and the implementation of district policy. To illustrate, is it ever desirable for a school principal to substitute personal judgment for district policy? The answer to that question is that it certainly is. The only thing that I insist on is that an administrator who does that has to play the game straight. If caught, the administrator has to live with the organizational penalties. That's the first caveat.

"The second is that any administrator who does not agree with the school district's policy should be upfront about it. There are no penalties attached to speaking up, to voicing disagreement, to asking for the consideration of other options, to working through the disagreements to some sort of mediated settlement. Generally, if an administrator is competent and upfront, supervisors will be tolerant of some creative insubordination. If it becomes a way of life, then I think that invokes another set of value problems, even for a competent administrator. One can't be at home in an organization unless there is alignment between the individual and the organization on basic values.

"I am certain you are all prepared and eager to assume an administrative post. I wish you success in your career goals, whether you pursue them in the Edgewood Community Schools or another school or school district. In just a few minutes, each of you will be given a certificate that notes you have completed this program. Before we do that, does anyone have any questions about my comments regarding culture building and the values that good administrators should exemplify?"

CASE 7.8: STUDENT DRESS AND SCHOOL DISTRICT VALUES

Danny Joe Price, assistant principal of Perry Senior High School, received a call from Frank Anderson, director of student services for the school district, early on Tuesday morning. Frank called to gather information about how Perry Senior High School was enforcing one of the current school board policies related to appropriate student dress. The policy stated that students were not permitted to wear clothing that advertised alcohol or drugs. Because the policy was not part of the discipline code for the district, violations carried no required punishment. Instead, each principal could decide how to handle violators.

"Yesterday afternoon at the school board meeting, board member Ray Torres requested information about the policy. Someone had complained to him that she saw a group of high school students wearing shirts with beer logos."

"That wouldn't have been our students, Frank," Danny Joe responded. "Most of our students have been pretty cooperative about complying with the district policy on dress."

"I'm sure you're right, Danny, but I didn't call to track down whether your students were involved. I'm really more interested in whether the current policy is difficult to enforce and, if so, what problems you have had with it. I'm in the process of calling all the high schools and junior high schools, just to gather information, you know."

"In other words, a board member asks a question, and everyone in the school district jumps."

"I agree, it seems that way sometimes, but Torres is on a real crusade. He suggested a three-day in-school suspension for students who wear T-shirts or other clothing with logos that advertise alcohol, beer, or tobacco. He made an impassioned plea that drug and alcohol abuse is the greatest problem facing the schoolchildren of today."

"Perhaps his statement is motivated more by his campaign for election to the state legislature than his commitment to children, Frank. I see this as a very minor offense and usually just ask the kids to turn their shirts inside out. Never had a kid refuse or a repeat offender."

"Other board members apparently agree with you and expressed a concern that by requiring a specific punishment, Torres's recommendation would make the rule part of the discipline code and increase the number of due process hearings."

"I couldn't support a three-day suspension," Danny Joe replied. "I think the problem is simply a distraction, something for the principal or teacher to deal with, much like a student tapping a pencil or talking in class."

"I think I understand your position, Danny. Thanks for your help."

Several days later, Danny Joe noticed an article in the local newspaper reporting on a campaign appearance that Ray Torres made at a high school in a neighboring school district. Torres had been questioned repeatedly by students regarding his proposal to penalize students for wearing clothes that advertise alcohol or drugs.

The reporter had included a lengthy statement by Torres in the story that ended with these words: "As a human services worker, I have seen how alcohol abuse affects people. Advertisements that send a message to 'drink and be merry' perpetuate a dangerous myth. We have a responsibility in the community to project a consistent message. District policy states that illegal chemicals are neither allowed nor promoted in the public schools. Students should not be allowed to test the limits. If we permit students to wear shirts that promote alcohol, we are saying that we approve. We don't. I don't. That's why I brought this up."

At the next school board meeting, the Torres motion to amend the dress code was defeated by a vote of 6 to 1.

CASE 7.9: THE INTERLOPERS AT WESTERN HILLS HIGH SCHOOL

Monmouth Park was an affluent, wooded suburb just outside a large industrial city. Over the years, growth had expanded the boundaries of the two until it was difficult to tell where the city ended and the suburb started. As suburban growth accelerated, Monmouth Park Independent School District had constructed several elementary schools, a middle school, and a high school to accommodate the subdivisions that had sprung up in the truck farming areas that once separated the city and the suburb.

The district had developed a reputation for quality education. The high schools had a high percentage of merit scholars, many advanced placement classes, and a tradition of academic and athletic excellence. Teachers who had once sought positions in the city now preferred the suburb because of higher salaries, less stressful environment, and a more supportive community.

Western Hills High School had been built so close to the municipal boundaries that it was less than a ten-minute walk from the last subway stop in the city to the campus of Western Hills. This proximity had precipitated problems for Monmouth Park school administrators. Superintendent of Schools Dr. Dan Ferth had scheduled a meeting with several other administrators to discuss one of these problems.

Paul Berrigan, principal of Western Hills, began the meeting by describing the problem. "The information you received, Dr. Ferth, appears to be correct. I had our attendance officer run a quick check, and at least two of the students currently enrolled at Western Hills are residents of the city, not our district. Who knows how many other illegally enrolled students we have. Both of the students we have identified are minorities, in advanced placement classes, the sort we're proud to claim as students."

"Well, in one respect I'm pleased that my information was accurate,"

Dr. Ferth replied. "It's nice to know that good students want to attend Monmouth schools, but the problem is that we have no local tax dollars supporting them. How did they get enrolled to begin with?"

"I can answer that," began Nichole Simmons, director of pupil personnel. "After your phone call, our office began investigating. We interviewed both of the Western Hills students who had been identified by Paul, and we discovered that each had provided an authentic address within the school district. The only hitch was that neither was living at the address given. We found out that both students reside in the central city and were riding the subway to the end of the line and then walking to the high school campus. Based on that, we've stationed several of our attendance officers at the subway stop and have, in fact, identified several other students who may be doing the same thing. Of course, we're checking it out. We suspect there may be some elementary students involved. One of my people talked to a fifth-grade girl who said she gets up at five o'clock in the morning to catch the subway."

"You know, this really bothers me," Paul interjected. "These kids are good students; they want to attend our schools; we want to have them. They haven't had many chances to succeed. Both of the kids at my school come from single-parent families, no money, no hope of doing better without a good education. I understand, I guess, why we have to try to identify these kids and remove them, but I really don't like it. Another thing. We know we continue to have some parents who provide false addresses in order to get their children enrolled in our district. What's different here is that education is so important to these kids that they're doing it on their own . . . and that they're minorities. Are we operating on a double standard?"

"I understand what you're saying, Paul," Dr. Ferth replied, "but we have to remember that we have an obligation to serve the children of our taxpayers. Our per pupil expenditures are among the highest in the state, and because of our high tax base, we qualify for very little state support. Our citizens are becoming aware of this problem, and I've been getting a little heat. I'm afraid if we don't stop it now, the situation will get nasty. Because most of the children involved are likely to be minorities, we have some racists in this community who might take this on as an issue."

"I've come up with a couple of ways to help these students without putting the school district in a difficult position," Nichole said. "For example, a few years ago we talked about an exchange program with the city schools. They have technical programs that some of our students would be interested in. Or we could provide nonresident tuition scholarships for a small number of highly qualified students."

Superintendent Ferth shook his head. "Those are both good ideas, Nichole, but I don't think this community is ready for either one. People moved here to get away from the city. Now they see the problems of the city coming to them. More important, the financial support isn't there. The children from the city we're talking about couldn't afford to come here without some kind of support or help, and our taxpayers aren't going to be willing to provide that. Even if these children could pay their own tuition, I'm not sure our community would support accepting them as students. We've been barely able to keep up with the growth in our community. As you know, we currently have a policy of refusing tuition students for just that reason."

"So what do we do?" Paul asked.

"What we've been doing," Dr. Ferth replied. "We continue our efforts to guarantee that all of our students are legitimate residents of this school district. We have no other choice."

"Okay, but I'll have a hard time explaining this to the two students at my school. They are at Western Hills because they want a good education. And now I'm going to tell them that we can't help them."

CASE 7.10: HIRING A SECRETARY
FOR THE BOARD PRESIDENT

Dominic Agnew, president of the school board for the Jackson County School District, opened discussion about the next item on the agenda. "It has been moved and seconded that the board hire a secretary who will be assigned to the board president. Is there any discussion?"

Reginald Newmann began: "I have several concerns that I would like to express. First, each school board member should have access to the talents of this person. Second, what will the selection process be? The superintendent by law must recommend a prospective employee to the board, and I would hope that the board would have the opportunity to approve or disapprove that person. This should not be something left totally within the president's authority, with all due respect to the president."

"Has the need for this position been established?" asked Parker Chamberlain. "Has it been established that we can't cover this need by reassigning people already working in our system? We've been talking about holding the line on budgetary matters. Now I realize the demands on the board president are very heavy. Some of us can use our business secretaries for doing school board work, but others are not able to do this. Does anyone want to speak for the need for this position?"

Richard Mathias replied. "There's no question about the need. When I was board president, my wife got sick and tired of doing work that we had to do together just to keep up with things. In Mr. Agnew's case, we can try to call his office, but we have great difficulty getting through, and Mr. Agnew has told me several times that it's impossible for him to continue to expect his secretary to handle both the business of the office and the school board business. I do think we should be able to share this secretary. She should have an automobile, and she should be able to take dictation over at your place for a letter you might write, Mr. Chamberlain. That's one thing I'd want her to be able to do if I were board president and she were my secretary. She should attend these board meetings so that she can keep up-to-date on board business. I just wouldn't take the presidency of the board again without some help. It's just too much trouble to drive downtown to work with the secretaries in our central administrative offices. You need one in your place of business, mostly to answer the telephone."

"Has a job description been drawn up for this person?" asked Chamberlain. "Remember, I'm just interrogating you to ascertain what we're looking for. I know that before the load got so heavy we had an opportunity to get an aide for each one of us, but we didn't do it. My next question is, where would the person be located and to whom would that person report? I raise these questions now in order to get a better basis for supporting you, because I would hate for us to create a position without some good guidelines."

Charlotte Hoffman indicated that she wished to speak. "The resolution that appears in our agenda says that the president will be responsible for the work location, assignment of duties, and the supervision of the person hired. Our attorney says that if this secretary is hired through the usual administrative hiring procedure, she should be supervised in the same way. Does it make sense for her to be supervised and evaluated by the board president when she's really a school district employee?"

"I want to speak in support of this motion for the president," said Byron Monarch, "as well as for the other board members. I've been very disappointed with the amount of secretarial support I've received when I've asked for assistance. I made a legitimate request a couple of weeks ago, through the proper channels, and I was told by the person I was assigned to work through that she couldn't handle it because she works for the superintendent. I thought that was a disappointing reply."

Board President Agnew responded. "I would insist that this person be available to help all board members. I will personally donate an office in my business for this secretary, along with a typewriter and everything else that's needed. I would prefer that the school district furnish the telephone line. With the current construction projects and everything else going on in the school district, I received 46 phone calls today alone. Because we're not full-time legislators, we either have to be rich or work in some governmental institution that tolerates the number of phone calls that a board member gets. I'm not complaining; I just believe that if one of you becomes board president, you would want some additional assistance to do the job well. I will be happy, however, to yield to the decision of this board."

"I would like to amend the motion," said board member Newmann. "I move we strike the words 'assigned to the president' and say 'assigned to the school board' and to insert 'with the advice and counsel of the school board' to indicate that the president has responsibility to work with the board in this matter."

"I see nothing to be accomplished by this amendment," responded Byron Monarch. "We already have secretaries who are supposedly assigned to the school board. The intent of this motion was to assign someone specifically to the board president."

Jack Oaks, also a former president of the board, finally entered the discussion. "I need some clarification. What does the maker of the amendment envision as far as office location and so forth?"

"My personal thought on this," began Reginald Newmann, "is that the person should be housed in the school board building, but that is a matter to be determined by the board. I don't want to see us get into a situation where there is so much autonomy and power placed in a single position that any of us feels some discomfort. The president has historically acted with the advice of the board, and I don't want us to change that."

"I have some mixed feelings about this," added Jack Oaks. "There is no doubt that duties have increased and will continue to increase and that some clerical assistance is warranted. I have some problems with locating the secretary anywhere but on school property, and that's why I ask my question. Would it work, Mr. Agnew, to house this person at some place other than your place of business?"

"Mr. Oaks, it would be of some assistance, and it might in fact work, but it would be very inefficient. I'd have to move to the administrative offices."

"Well that's possible, too, Mr. Agnew," replied Oaks, and the other board members laughed at the joke.

"Well, I've been through that one too," Agnew responded. "One way or another, I've got to have some relief. The baby needs milk today."

Jack Oaks was nearly ready to vote on the issue. "Your personal situation lends itself to this proposal. Some of us, no doubt, could do the same thing, but Mr. Mathias, for example, probably would not have wanted a full-time secretary located in his home."

"My wife did," replied Mathias, as the board members laughed.

"Well maybe you would have," responded Oaks, "but it would have been very difficult for me. I really want to support this motion, but I have a problem with the location of the secretary."

"I've checked with our attorney," Chamberlain added, "and he informs me that there are no legal problems with the president having a secretary located at his place of business. The secretary should be where the person is performing his work, and I have no problem with that. I was happy to hear, Mr. Agnew, that you said you will yield to the decision of this board. I'm delighted that you have *finally* concluded that you should yield to the decision of this board. There's no conflict, as I see it, because there are no legal implications."

"Are we ready to vote?" President Agnew asked.

In the voting that followed, the amendment proposed by Newmann failed and the original motion passed by a vote of 6 to 1.

CASE 7.11: CHOOSING THE CHEERLEADING SQUAD

Rhonda Winship had been coach of the cheerleading squads at Kennedy Senior High School for over 15 years, and she had never before faced a problem quite like this. Each year late in the spring semester tryouts were held to select cheerleaders for the next year's squads.

Kennedy was a multi-ethnic, multi-racial urban school. Twenty-five percent of the students were black, 1.3 percent were Hispanic, and 3.2 percent were Asians. In the current school year, the cheerleading squads reflected the diversity of the student body. The varsity squad had one black girl, two Asians, and five Caucasians. The junior varsity squad was composed of two blacks and six Caucasians. The sophomore squad was two blacks, one Asian, and five Caucasians.

The practice had been to make contact with the junior high schools in order to select the tenth-grade squad for the next year. An elaborate selection procedure developed for use with the varsity squad was also used for the prospective tenth graders. Attendance and tardiness records for the girls were supplied by the junior high administrators. Counselors provided information about grades and gave a citizenship rating to each girl. At the time of the tryouts, each girl had to be passing all subjects. During the two-week practice period, current cheerleaders worked with the girls who were trying out for the squad. The girls tried out in sets of three, and they arranged their groups for the tryouts so that they could practice together.

Of the 25 girls who actually tried out for the tenth-grade squad, 18 were white, 7 were black, 2 were Hispanic, and 2 were Asians. Ten girls were to be selected. Rhonda had invited a panel to judge the tryouts, including current cheerleaders, several teachers, two cheerleading sponsors from the junior high schools, and high school students. Only 3 of the 5 blacks she asked to serve on the panel showed up for the tryouts.

Tryouts were held before the judges only. The doors of the gymnasium were locked to keep out friends and family. Rhonda had always felt that it would be unfair if some girls had supporters and others had none. Judges were given evaluation sheets which asked for a rating in each of 15 categories. Rhonda had asked the teachers on the judging panel to tally up the scores because she believed she could trust them to keep the individual scores confidential. As she looked over the tally sheets, she noticed that all ten of the girls selected were white. It was nearly ten o'clock at night before she announced the results to the girls, as she had promised, and that's when the problems started.

Following the procedures she had always used, participants were permitted to look at their individual ballots, though they could not see the judges' names or the scores of the other girls. The ten girls chosen were listed in alphabetical order, but the rankings within the top ten were not disclosed. Several of the black girls had reacted very strongly when the results were announced. They said the tryouts had not been fair because no black girls had been named to the squad. One stormed out of the gymnasium in tears, and two others asked to look at the results and afterwards seemed more satisfied.

By midmorning the next day, Rhonda had received several phone calls, some threatening, some accusing, all from people upset about the tryout results. A few threatened to contact a local black legislator who was a strong advocate for the black community. Others threatened to get her fired. Some accused her of having the current cheerleaders work more with the white girls than the black girls during the two-week practice period. By early afternoon Rhonda decided to contact Cynthia Brooks, a black assistant principal at Kennedy. "Cynthia," she said, "I've had very few parent challenges to the selection process in the past. When I have had some complaints, I've shown the ballots to the concerned parents and that satisfied them."

Cynthia had been very calm. "These things happen," she had said, "but you should let the principal know. If I were Cecil Cross, I'd want to know."

Cross was in his office when Rhonda stopped by to see him. He looked exasperated when she explained to him what had happened with the tryouts for the tenth-grade cheering squad. "This will certainly cause some political unrest in the community," he said. He then asked to see all of the rating sheets and summary results. He told Rhonda he would like to meet with her to discuss the results the next day, once he had a chance to examine them.

The meeting was scheduled for the next morning before school. The first statement Cross made was, "I can see no bias reflected in the results. I notice, however, that several black girls lost points because of attendance and citizenship. You know, you should have recruited more blacks as judges, even if you had to go through the school halls at the last minute to draft some people who could help out. The bottom line is that we have to do something to change the results. Let's meet again later today."

Case 7.11: Part Two

Tension in the girls' athletic area remained high during the day. Rhonda was still receiving telephone calls from parents and community members, some insisting that the process had been unfair and some commending her for the selections. She noticed that the cheerleaders spent a lot of time hanging around the locker room and conferring with each other.

When she met with Cross later that day, he said that when he had come into the school district as a new assistant principal three years earlier, he had noticed what he described as "a low representation of blacks" on the cheerleading squads. He told Rhonda that she should make more of an effort to recruit black girls. He had looked at the data from the tryouts and decided that the two black girls who had ranked highest among the alternates should be added to the squad. These two girls had scores very close to those of the ten who had been selected; the other black girls had received much lower scores. Cross told Rhonda to call all the parents of the girls who had been selected to tell them that he and the administration had decided to add two girls. He told her, "Don't try to explain how or why the action is being taken."

He then told Rhonda to develop a plan for future selection of cheerleading squads which would establish racial quotas. She was to bring the plan back to Cross for approval within a month.

She asked him whether the same quotas would be applied to the boys' and girls' basketball teams, which had always had a majority of black players, and the tennis team, which had always been white. She reminded him that there was no quota system for selection to any of the sports teams or any other organized school activity of which she was aware. Even the flap two years before when a black student had narrowly missed being named to the National Honor Society had not resulted in quotas for students named to the group. Parents had raised a fuss then that was no more acerbic than the current concern about the cheerleaders.

Cross made it clear he didn't want to discuss the matter further. She left his office, angry and hurt that a decision she could not support was being forced on her.

Case 7.11: Part Three

As word about the two additional cheerleaders on the tenth-grade squad spread through Kennedy, she noticed that the cheerleaders seemed agitated and upset. Finally, several of the varsity squad members showed up in her office. They told her that they didn't think adding girls to the squad was fair, and they asked for an explanation.

She tried to explain as best she could without giving them the reason the decision had been made. One of them finally said, "It's because they're black, Mrs. Winship, isn't it?" She didn't like being evasive, but she didn't respond. The girls wanted to know whose decision it was and added, "We know it wasn't you, Mrs. Winship, because you're fair."

Rhonda told them that two more girls would now have the chance to learn and that the sophomore squad was a training ground for future squads. She reminded them that any selection process needed at times to be changed. When they left her office, they seemed to understand that they had to accept the decision.

Though Cross had asked her not to talk to the faculty about the decision, she confided later that day in two teachers who had been on the panel of judges. She felt they deserved an explanation for why twelve names were announced when the panel had selected only ten girls.

Case 7.11: Part Four

The problems at Kennedy seemed to be over when two weeks later Rhonda learned from Cynthia Brooks that some members of the black community had called the office of Isaiah Robinson, a black assistant superintendent for community relations. Rhonda reported that to Cross immediately. He told her that she didn't need to be concerned. She could call Robinson if she wanted, but she certainly wasn't obligated to do so.

She called Robinson and talked to him on the telephone. He told her that a group of parents had contacted him about some concerns, one of which might be cheerleading. He said he planned to meet with the group next week. Rhonda asked Robinson whether she should plan to come to that meeting and volunteered to be in the central office and available with the selection results should questions about the cheerleading tryouts arise. Robinson told her that it wasn't necessary that she do that. He said, "You know, you need to be fair, and the black community needs to be represented. If cheerleaders are picked and blacks aren't represented, then something is wrong."

In the course of their conversation, Robinson pointed out that during the Kennedy cheerleader tryouts, one black girl had jumped very well and not made the squad while one white girl who had made the squad had not jumped well. It became obvious to Rhonda that someone had been talking to him.

When she hung up the telephone, Rhonda felt overwhelmed. She wasn't sure how long she could put up with these innuendoes about unfairness when she had always seen herself as very fair.

Rhonda had coached cheerleading at Kennedy for 17 years, and she regularly coached or assisted with seven other school activities. She had more than pulled her weight at Kennedy. She had planned to resign as cheerleading coach at the end of the school year. Now, because of this problem with the tenth-grade squad, she no longer felt she could do that. She was sure that it would appear as if the problem were the reason for her resignation. She also suspected that Cross would hold it against her if she resigned. She was scheduled to be one of the tenured faculty evaluated during the next school year. She felt victimized and trapped.

CASE 7.12: CELEBRATING THE HOLIDAY SEASON

Katie Novatny, principal of Perry Junior High School, always looked forward to the holiday season. As she walked by the music practice rooms, she heard the children singing traditional Christmas music. She hadn't found many opportunities to visit the music area this semester, so she decided to stop for a few minutes to enjoy the music.

As she sat in the back of the room for several minutes and shuffled through a stack of music that had been left on a chair, she was reminded that she had neglected to talk to Roger Florey, the new vocal music director, about the upcoming holiday concert. The music she was hearing and the music she had looked at were both religious, and that was going to be a problem.

Katie waited until the end of the rehearsal. As the students filed out, she walked to the front of the room to talk to Roger. "Roger," she began, "the students sound great. You're doing a fine job with them, but I'm afraid we have a problem here."

"Thanks, I think the kids sound good, too, Katie. What's the problem?"

"Well, let me explain it this way. Up until last year our community has always observed Christmas in very traditional ways. We followed the Christian traditions in the schools—Christmas trees, carols, a nativity scene, the whole thing. But last year the parents of two Jewish children, one of whom was a student here at Perry, enlisted the support of the American Civil Liberties Union and sued the school district. They argued that the schools permitted prayers to be read at school assemblies during the holiday season and allowed religious carols such as 'Silent Night' to be sung at public events and assemblies."

"I didn't know that. What happened?"

"The federal district court judge ruled that the prayers were inappropriate but that the religious songs, when sung as part of a traditional holiday celebration, have primarily a secular purpose."

"That's a relief, Katie. I thought you were about to tell me that I need to change my whole program to get rid of the religious songs."

"I think you should make some changes, Roger. From what I've heard and seen, I'd say that most of the music you're planning to use is religious. Our new school district guidelines for the celebration of holidays say that a school program or student performance should not be a forum for religious worship."

"Well, I never intended the program to be that."

"But, Roger, it could be interpreted that way. Our community is changing. We need to ensure that our school programs are inclusive and pluralistic. Could the Steinberg children, for example, comfortably perform in your concert? What about the Cheung children?"

"Ross Steinberg can't carry a tune in a bucket and Sang Cheung barely speaks English, you know. I understand your point, Katie, but those are only two families. We have nine hundred children in this school. After all, Christmas is a religious holiday, one based on the Christian ethic that is part of the foundation of this country. It seems to me that most of the community wants a traditional celebration. From what I understand, you've had standing-room-only audiences. The judge's decision supports us. Why should we change?"

"What about adding some traditional, secular songs to the performance?"

"We could do that, I suppose. In fact, the kids have been practicing 'Frosty, the Snow Man.' We could include that, and I'm sure I can come up with a couple of others. I just think that you're overreacting."

"That's all I'm asking, Roger. Do what you can. Next year maybe we should plan for a winter concert sometime other than the third week in December."

"Whatever you say, Katie. You're the boss."

Katie chuckled as she walked out of the room. "Boss" was not a word she ever thought about in reference to herself.

References

Culbertson, J. A. (1964). The preparation of administrators. In D. E. Griffiths (Ed.), *Behavioral science and educational administration*. The 63rd Yearbook of the National Society for the Study of Education (pp. 303–330). Chicago: National Society for the Study of Education.

Culbertson, J. A., Jacobson, P. A., & Reller, T. L. (1960). *Administrative relationships: A casebook*. Englewood Cliffs, NJ: Prentice-Hall.

Edge, A. G., & Coleman, D. R. (1978). *The guide to case analysis and reporting*. Honolulu: System Logistics, Inc.

Haller, E. J., & Strike, K. A. (1986). *An introduction to educational administration: Social, legal and ethical perspectives*. New York: Longman.

Kimbrough, R. B. (1985). *Ethics: A course of study for educational leaders*. Arlington, VA: American Association of School Administrators.

National Commission on Excellence in Educational Administration. (1987). *Leaders for America's schools*. Tempe, AZ: University Council for Educational Administration.

Robinson, G. M., & Moulton, J. (1985). *Ethical problems in higher education*. Englewood Cliffs, NJ: Prentice-Hall.

Schoen, D. A. (1987). *Educating the reflective practitioner*. San Francisco: Jossey-Bass.